Dark
Mysteries
of the
Vatican

Dark Mysteries of the Vatican

of the

Vatican

H. Paul Jeffers

CITADEL PRESS
Kensington Publishing Corp.
www.kensingtonbooks.com

CITADEL PRESS BOOKS are published by

Kensington Publishing Corp.
119 West 40th Street
New York, NY 10018

Copyright © 2010 H. Paul Jeffers

All Kensington titles, imprints, and distributed lines are available at special quantity discounts for bulk purchases for sales promotions, premiums, fund-raising, educational, or institutional use. Special book excerpts or customized printings can also be created to fit specific needs. For details, write or phone the office of the Kensington special sales manager: Kensington Publishing Corp., 119 West 40th Street, New York, NY 10018, attn: Special Sales Department; phone 1-800-221-2647.

CITADEL PRESS and the Citadel logo are Reg. U.S. Pat. & TM Off.

First printing: February 2010

10 9 8 7 6 5 4 3 2

Printed in the United States of America

Library of Congress Control Number: 2009937069

ISBN-13: 978-0-8065-3132-8
ISBN-10: 0-8065-3132-0

To Jennifer and Mark Nisbit

For there is nothing hid, which shall not be made manifest: neither was it made secret, but that it may come abroad.
—Jesus Christ (Matthew 4:22)

Contents

Introduction Keys to the Kingdom   1

1   Thou Shalt Not Read   5

2   The Truth About the Templars   15

3   Vatican Treasures   23

4   Naughty Priests   33

5   Murder in Holy Orders   41

6   The Mystery of the Pope's Banker   53

7   From Russia with Malice   61

8   Opus Dei: The Pope's Cult   73

9   The Papacy and the Nazis   83

10   Spooks and Rats   95

11   A Fit of Madness   105

12   Vatican Espionage   117

13   The Devil, You Say   123

14   Myths, Rumors, and Presidents   129

15   And God Created Aliens   135

16   The Vatican and the End of the World   143

Vatican Library Chronology   151

Vatican Archives Chronology   153

The Popes   155

Chinon Parchment   165

The Lateran Treaty of 1929 (excerpts)   177

Further Reading   183

Index   185

Dark
Mysteries
of the
Vatican

Introduction: Keys to the Kingdom

Almost from the moment Jesus Christ changed the fisherman Simon's name to Peter and gave him the keys to the kingdom of Heaven, the religion that was built in Christ's name began keeping secrets out of necessity. Deemed by the Roman emperors to be dangerous, Christians literally went underground by gathering to worship in catacombs and caves. They came up with secret hand signals, symbols, and other signs of recognition and means of communication to avoid detection and persecution. From its outset, Christianity was a religion of secrets.

After three centuries of suppression, the outlaw status of followers of Christ ended when the Emperor Constantine converted to the religion after literally seeing the light. While on the way to battle his most powerful rival, Maxentius, at the Tiber River in A.D. 312, "he reported seeing the cross of Christ superimposed on the sun with the words 'In hoc signo vinces' (In this sign you shall conquer)." He ordered his men to put crosses on their shields and won the battle. "The very next year, he met with Emperor Licinius, ruler of the Roman Empire's eastern provinces, to sign the Edict of Milan, giving equal rights to all religious groups within the Roman Empire. He returned property seized from Christians, built a large number of churches, donated land," sent his mother to Jerusalem to find the place where Christ was crucified and build a church on the spot, and ordered the bishops of the religion to convene in the "first Council of Nicaea in A.D. 325 to deal with false teaching within the church." Results of this conclave were a formal list of Christian beliefs (the Nicaean Creed) and approval of texts for inclusion in the Holy Bible.

1

In this process of "canonization," by which excluded texts were deemed to be heretical, the bishops who met at Nicaea claimed an absolute authority to decide what knowledge could be disseminated and what should be kept secret that the Roman Catholic Church continues to assert. When Constantine constructed the Basilica of St. Peter on Vatican Hill in the heart of Rome as the throne of Peter's successors, it became the Holy See.

The current location of St. Peter's Basilica is the site of the Circus of Nero in the first century. After Constantine officially recognized Christianity, he started construction (in 324) of a great basilica on the spot where tradition placed the crucifixion and burial of St. Peter. In the mid-fifteenth century, it was decided to rebuild the old basilica. Pope Nicholas V asked architect Bernardo Rossellino to start adding to the old church. Construction on the present building began under Pope Julius II in 1596 and was finished in 1615 under Pope Paul V. Surrounding structures that constitute Vatican City include buildings that house the Vatican Secret Archives.

As "defender of the faith" for more than sixteen centuries and the repository of the suppressed knowledge of centuries, the Vatican has become the focus of people who weave countless legends, myths, and tales of mysterious doings, sinister secrets, and dark criminal conspiracies concocted within its walls. Contributing to suspicions surrounding the Vatican is an aura of mystery that has surrounded the Roman Catholic Church for centuries, including use of Latin in ceremonies, secrecy in the selection of popes, symbolic robes and headpieces, rituals of worship, belief in miracles and apparitions of saints, and the Church's historic claim that in matters of faith the pope was infallible. All this left non-Catholics feeling that the Church was rooted in secrecy.

Nothing has been more fascinating to those who believe that the Vatican hides things than the Vatican Secret Archives. From the years immediately after the crucifixion of Jesus, popes carefully preserved manuscripts in the scrinium Sanctae Romanae Ecclesiae. Today the files of 264 popes and the Vatican hierarchy fill thirty miles of shelves of documents tied with red ribbon (the origin of the term "red tape"). Housed in Renaissance buildings not far from the Sistine Chapel in Vatican City in the heart of

Rome, there are files on not only the entire history of Christianity but on Western civilization. No one, including the pope, can state with certainty how many secrets and scandals lie in the archives. "The oldest document dates back to the end of the 7th century, while the archives have an almost uninterrupted documentation starting from 1198. The Secret Vatican Archives are primarily used by the Pope and his Curia, that is [the] Holy See. In 1881, under Pope Leo XIII, the Archives were opened to be freely consulted by scholars, thus becoming the most important center of historical research in the world."

Some material has been made available on the Internet. More than six hundred archival sources extending over more than fifty-two miles of shelves, covering over eight hundred years of history, can now be visited on the Vatican website (www.vatican.va).

"The oldest document dates back to the 7th century, while uninterrupted documentation is maintained from the year 1198 onward. . . . It is possible to see Michelangelo Buonarotti's letter to the Bishop of Cesena (January 1550), the minutes of the trial of Galileo (1616–33)," letters about Henry VIII and his desire to annul his marriage to Catherine of Aragon so he could wed Anne Boleyn, and the parchment in which Pope Clement V granted absolution to the leaders of the Knights Templar (August 17–20, 1308), after they were burned at the stake.

Widespread belief that the Vatican archives are crammed with dark secrets arose in 2003 with the publication of Dan Brown's novel *The Da Vinci Code* and later with the movie based on it. The fictional story presented an elaborate centuries-old plot by the Church dating to the years when the Knights Templar conspired with the Church to suppress proof that Jesus was married to Mary Magdalene, that they had a daughter, that the child was "the holy grail," that she was taken to France, and that her descendants, the bloodline of Christ, are walking around the world today. Although the facts contained in the novel have been subsequently exposed as false or misleading, the effect of the novel and movie has been to strengthen the belief that the Vatican will go to any length to keep its secrets from being revealed.

While *The Da Vinci Code* presented an imaginary conspiracy, the history of the Vatican is replete with actual events that the Holy See was eager to keep secret and with incidents that outsiders were just as eager to whip up into fantastic theories involving murder, poisoned popes, illicit sex, conniving with Nazis, Communist conspiracies, stolen gold and art treasures, and other nastiness in which the truth was suppressed.

Arranged chronologically and thematically, this book explores this fascinating saga of the dark secrets of the Vatican to sift fact from fable and illuminate the truth of what lies in the archives, from sexual escapades of popes and priests, murders in holy orders, financial scandal, and international intrigue to stories of UFOs, and prophecies about the end of the world.

CHAPTER 1

Thou Shalt Not Read

When movie director Ron Howard requested permission in 2008 to shoot scenes for *Angels & Demons*, the latest movie thriller by Dan Brown, that takes place in the Vatican and Rome's churches, Archbishop Velasio De Paolis, head of the Vatican's Prefecture for Economic Affairs, banned use of any Church property in Rome. He said that the author of *The Da Vinci Code* had "turned the gospels upside down to poison the faith."

Calling the best-selling novel's premise that Jesus and Mary Magdalene married and had a child "an offense against God," Da Paolis asserted, "It would be unacceptable to transform churches into film sets so that his blasphemous novels can be made into films in the name of business." He added that Brown's work "wounds common religious feelings."

"Father Marco Fibbi, spokesman for the Diocese of Rome, said, 'Normally we read the script but this time it was not necessary. The name Dan Brown was enough.'"

When the movie version of *The Da Vinci Code* was released, a top Vatican official urged all Roman Catholics to boycott it. Calling the book "stridently anti-Christian," Archbishop Angelo Amato, a close aide to Pope Benedict XVI, said it was "'full of calumnies, offenses and historical and theological errors regarding Jesus, the Gospels and the church.... If such lies and errors had been directed at the Koran or the Holocaust, they would have justly provoked a world uprising.... Instead, if they were directed against the Catholic Church and Christians, they remained unpunished."

As the second-ranking official in the Vatican's doctrinal office, Amato urged a boycott similar to the one in 1988 against *The Last Temptation of Christ*, directed by Martin Scorsese. When *The Da Vinci Code* was published in 2003, Catholic leaders and some other Christians were outspoken against it. In the weeks before the film was released, Opus Dei, the lay Catholic group whose members were portrayed as villains in the story, sponsored forums and other public events to refute the book's premise and dispute its suggestions that the group is shadowy and secretive.

Banning Howard from filming *Angels & Demons* in any of Rome's churches and at the Vatican and the earlier protests against Brown's book and its film version were echoes of a time when the Vatican exercised unquestionable power to control dissemination of knowledge in books that was made possible by means of printing presses using moveable type. Invented by Johann Gutenberg in 1454, the press revolutionized the world of religion by making the Bible widely available, and introducing printed books to the world.

This proliferation of published material resulted in an effort by the Vatican to dictate what Catholics could read. It did so by establishing the *Index Librorum Prohibitorum (The Index of Prohibited Books)*. "Active from 1559 until 1966, the [Index] listed books that Catholics should neither own nor read under pain of excommunication.

"During the Index's long life," noted an article in *America, the National Catholic Weekly*, "the public was told about the latest bans, but not the reasons for them. Behind closed doors, though, the Vatican officials held long and sometimes heated debates about the books of the day." After more than a decade of studying the Index, a diocesan priest and history professor at Münster University in Germany, the Reverend Hubert Wolf stated, "Nowhere else in the world did an institution try to control the medium of modern times, the book, for over 400 years."

The archives covering Church debates about thousands of books offer a unique insight into centuries of Vatican thinking on theology, philosophy, history, politics, science, and world literature. Stored in a basement of what was once known as the Holy Office, now called the Congregation for the Doctrine of the Faith, the files were closed to outside researchers for centuries. Building the archives started in earnest with the Inquisition in 1542 to combat the Protestant Reformation that began with Martin Luther's challenge to papal authority. After he nailed his "95 theses" to the church door in Wittenberg, Germany, in 1515, they were printed in Leipzig, Nuremberg, and Basel and distributed widely. The Holy Office was soon overwhelmed by the combination of the printing press and prolific Protestant authors who employed it to foster a publishing explosion as influential in its time as the Internet is today. The Vatican established a separate office, the Congregation of the Index, to deal just with books in 1571.

"The first Index,...published in 1559, banned all books by Luther, John Calvin and other Protestant reformers. Since translating the Holy Bible into vernacular language was a Protestant specialty, all Bibles but the Roman Catholic Latin Vulgate were banned. The Talmud and the Koran were also taboo." The *Index* also listed "books that should be purged of passages that were in conflict with Church teaching. Classical writers— including Plato, Aristotle, Cicero, Virgil, Homer, Euclid, Hippocrates, Thucydides and others—were put on the *expurgatio* list because they reflected pagan beliefs. Books translated by Protestants had to be filtered for offending passages. In some cases, a book only had to be printed in a 'Protestant' city to earn a place on the list of objectionable works...."

The Index Congregation met three or four times a year in Rome. Two "consultors" were named for each book being surveyed. Their findings were discussed at a meeting of cardinals in the congregation. The congregation's decision was then brought to the pope for approval. This produced a vast accumulation of files, written in Latin or Italian and divided into the *Diarii*, which recorded the congregation's sessions, and the *Protocolli*, with all kinds of other papers. The Inquisition congregation met weekly but handled only 2 or 3 percent of the censorship cases, usually theology books.

"Over the centuries, the Index managed to condemn a large number of writings that eventually became classics of European culture. Banned philosophy books included works by Descartes, Spinoza, Locke, Hume, Rousseau, Voltaire, Pascal, Kant and Mill. Among the novelists listed were Balzac, Flaubert, Hugo, Zola, D'Annunzio and Moravia. Books by the novelists Daniel Defoe and Jonathan Swift were blacklisted. The censors' zeal varied over the years and lost steam as the 20th century wore on. One of their last targets was [Jean Paul] Sartre, whose complete works were banned as early as 1948."

Suppression of "forbidden books" began with a conference on the contents of the Holy Bible for Christians in A.D. 393 at which the church elders compiled the Old Testament and the "approved" gospels of Mark, Matthew, Luke, and John; the book of Revelations; letters of Peter and Paul; and the Acts of the Apostles. With all other texts banned, the Church began sixteen centuries of forbidding possession and reading of disapproved books and accumulation of a Vatican library of literature that was forbidden to Catholics. "Ever since St. Paul's new converts at Ephesus burned their old magic books, the Church has waged war against books that might damage the faith or morals of its communicants."

The Index "listed books which Catholics were not to read. They included non-Catholic editions of the Bible, books attacking Catholic dogma, those defending 'heresy or schism,' and those which 'discuss, describe or teach impure or obscene matters,' such as *Lady Chatterley's Lover*." However, "any Catholic with a 'good reason' for reading a banned book could get permission from his bishop. Many U.S. bishops give temporary blanket permissions to students to read books necessary for their studies." Although the Vatican no longer issues an Index, the Church continues to condemn books, along with films, that are either contrary to Christian doctrine or offensive to the Church and morally wrong.

This militant stance frequently resulted in a desire by some authors to have their books "banned in Boston" in the belief that official disapproval by the Catholic Church would produce brisk sales among non-Catholics. Condemnation of *The Da Vinci Code*, and all the resulting controversial publicity, contributed to the novel's phenomenal commercial success.

After centuries of screening books for Christian orthodoxy and moral acceptability, the Vatican accumulated the world's largest collection of religiously and morally condemned books and manuscripts. But the Vatican Library is also the repository of volumes of science, history, and philosophy dating to the Middle Ages and earlier. The present library was founded in

1451 by Pope Nicholas V (1147–1455). Eugene IV bequeathed 340 manuscripts and Nicholas V added his own collection to form the basis of the library. A century before printing, he increased the holdings by employing monks to copy manuscripts that could not be bought from their owners. He also gathered materials that had belonged to the Imperial Library at Constantinople after the city fell to the Byzantines. When Nicholas died, he had increased the library to 1,200 manuscripts. When Pope Sixtus IV (1471–84) housed the library in the Vatican Palace, it became known as the Palatine Library. Today the Vatican Library is open to scholars and academics who submit a letter of accreditation from a university or research institute. Its collection consists of about 1.6 million volumes, including some 75,000 manuscripts and 8,300 incunabula (printed books from the second half of the fifteenth century).

"The Vatican Secret Archives have been estimated to contain fifty-two miles of shelving, and there are 35,000 volumes in the selective catalogue alone. 'Publication of the indexes, in part or as a whole, is forbidden,' according to the regulations current in 2005." According to the Vatican website, the oldest surviving document dates back to the end of the eighth century. Movement of the material from one location to another, and political upheavals, nearly "caused the total loss of all the archival material preceding [the reign of] Pope Innocent III. From 1198 onward more complete archives exist, although documentation is scarce before the 13th century." Of most interest to historians are documents related to the Inquisition.

"The Inquisition itself was established by Pope Gregory IX in 1233 as a special court to help curb the influence of heresy. It escalated as Church officials began to rely on civil authorities to fine, imprison, and even torture heretics. It reached its height in the 16th century to counter the spread of the Protestant Reformation. The department later became the Holy Office and its successor is now called the Congregation for the Doctrine of the Faith, which controls the orthodoxy of Roman Catholic teaching. Its [former] head, Cardinal Joseph Ratzinger, now Pope Benedict XVI, declared the archives open at a special conference at which he recalled how the decision stemmed from a letter written to Pope John Paul II...

by Carlo Ginzburg, a Jewish-born, atheist professor in Los Angeles. [The Pope wrote,] 'I am sure that opening our archives will respond not just to the legitimate aspirations of scholars but also the Church's firm intention to serve man helping him to understand himself by reading without prejudice his own history.' "

Arguably the most infamous trial of the Inquisition was that of the astronomer Galileo Galilei. Born in 1574 in Pisa, Italy, he was determined to study medicine. He enrolled at the University of Pisa in 1581, but soon switched his scientific interests to study mathematics and physics. Among his experiments, it is said (but not confirmed), was taking his pulse to time the swings of a lamp hanging from a ceiling of the Pisa cathedral. In his subsequent experiments, he described the physics of the pendulum. By dropping balls of varying weights from the Tower of Pisa, he found that they fell with equal velocity and uniform acceleration.

Forced because of financial reasons to leave the university without earning a degree, he returned to Florence, but eventually went back to the university as a teacher and became a lively participant in campus disputes and controversies. That there was a rebel within Galileo came to the attention of the faculty and students when he mocked the custom of wearing academic robes by declaring that they would be better to abandon clothing altogether.

After the death of his father in 1591 left him responsible for supporting his mother and siblings, he accepted a more remunerative post at the University of Padua.

Remaining there for eighteen years, he continued work in the area of motion, while widening his interests into astronomy by modifying a simple telescope into one that allowed him to study the mountains of the Moon, the phases of Venus, the moons of Jupiter, spots on the surface of the Sun, and the stars of the Milky Way. By publishing his findings in a booklet titled *The Starry Messenger*, he found that his scientific reputation rose like a skyrocket. But his further observations resulted in interest in theories proposed in 1543 by Nicholas Copernicus that the Sun was the center of the universe and that the Earth was a rotating planet that revolved around it.

By embracing Copernicus, Galileo placed himself in conflict with the Church's doctrine of Creation, based on the Bible's account in Genesis. Known as geocentrism, it fixed Earth in the center of the universe with the Sun and stars circling it. Declaring the Copernican view dangerous to the faith in 1616, the Church summoned Galileo to the city of Rome. His "instruction" from Cardinal Robert Bellarmine was to not "hold, teach and defend in any manner whatsoever, in words or in print" the Copernican doctrine. It was a sobering warning. But four years later, Galileo learned that the pope, Urban VIII, had declared that "the Holy Church had never, and never would, condemn" Copernicanism as heretical, but "only as rash, though there was no danger that anyone would ever demonstrate it to be necessarily true."

Interpreting this as indirect permission to continue with his explorations of the Copernican view, Galileo plunged into six years of study. The result was a vigorous defense of Copernicus in *Dialogue Concerning the Two Chief World Systems*. By publishing it, Galileo found himself in Rome again on the charge of defying Cardinal Bellarmine's instruction not to defend Copernicus in any way. The trial by a panel of cardinals began in the fall of 1632.

When the inquiry ended a year later, the Church pronounced and declared that Galileo was "suspect of heresy" for having held and believed the "false doctrine" that the Earth was not the center of the universe. The cardinals informed Galileo, who was now seventy years old, that the Holy Office was willing to absolve him, provided that first, "with sincere heart and unfeigned faith, in our presence you adjure [recant], curse and detest the said errors and heresies." Declaring the *Dialogue* prohibited, the panel of judges condemned him to "imprisonment in the Holy Office at our pleasure." But they reserved "the power of moderating, commuting, or taking off" the sentence. What they might do depended on whether Galileo knelt before them to recant.

Admitting on June 21, 1633, that he had defied the warning not to speak or write in defense of Copernicus, he said, "I abjure with a sincere heart deigned faith those errors and heresies, and I curse and detest them

[and] I swear that for the future I shall neither say nor assert orally or in writing such as may bring upon me similar suspicions."

After a period of confinement, Galileo was allowed go to his home near Florence, where he lived in seclusion in failing health and going nearly blind. He died on January 8, 1642.

Accounts of his submission to the Church, published more than a century later, contain a statement that may be a legend. As he rose from his knees after recanting, he may or may not have said quietly in Italian, "Eppur si mouve." (Nevertheless, it [the earth] does move.)

In November 1992, at a ceremony in Rome, before the Pontifical Academy of Sciences, Pope John Paul II officially declared that Galileo was right. The formal rehabilitation was based on the findings of a committee of the Academy the pope set up in 1979, soon after taking office. The committee decided the Inquisition had acted in good faith, but was wrong. Today the Vatican has its own celestial observatory.

The Vatican noted that archives of the Inquisition and *Index* had not survived well through the centuries. Because the "Church had a tradition of burning many of the most delicate heresy files," and the Inquisition's archive was almost entirely burned on Pope Paul IV's death in 1559, many documents had been lost. Some "were hauled off to Paris under Napoleon's rule in 1810 . . . and more than 2,000 volumes were burned. Some fell into rivers during transit, others were sold for paper or became mixed up with other files." Today the Vatican possesses "around 4,500 volumes, of which only a small part refer to the heresy trials. The rest deal with theological controversies and spiritual questions."

A book that was never banned by the Church is Charles Darwin's *The Origin of Species*, which is the basis of the theory of evolution. Unlike some Protestant fundamentalist churches that take the Bible literally on the subject of God creating mankind, the Earth, and the universe in seven days, the Vatican has recently stated that it is possible that some species, with the assistance of a higher power, were able to evolve into the species that exist in the world today.

Reporting on the opening of an exhibit of Vatican Archive material in 2008, *Newsweek* magazine noted that the display included "documents about the Church's restrictions on the movement of Jews, instructions for persecuting Protestants.... There were 18th-century maps outlining the ghettos of Rome, Ancona and Ferrara, depicting where Jews could live in pink or yellow and where they were allowed to keep businesses in blue. There were documents with handwritten regulations describing when Jewish women could be out of the gated areas and what they could wear. There were sketches of prisons and extensive lists of banned books and written edicts.... One from 1611 outlined how inquisitors should comport themselves both on the job and off and an illustration showing what their children should wear to school and to the beach. Investigators were even told what pajamas were acceptable.

"Other documents targeted game hunters and fishermen who were thought to be poaching from Vatican grounds. And then there's a gem-encrusted pastoral staff taken in the nineteenth century from a man who was condemned to death for claiming he was a saint. Inquisitors had authority in areas ranging from iconography and the way images of saints and prelates could be portrayed.

"This wasn't the first time that the Church tried to show that the judges of the Inquisition were not as brutal as previously believed. In 2004, the Vatican published an 800-page report claiming that of those investigated as heretics by the notorious Spanish Inquisition, which was independent of Rome in the fifteenth century, only 1.8 percent of the accused were actually executed. Nonetheless, Pope John Paul II referred to the Church's 700-year campaign against heresy as a 'tormented phase' and the 'greatest error in the Church's history.' "

One book that was not banned was the classic nineteenth-century novel *Uncle Tom's Cabin* by Harriet Beecher Stowe. While it was being scrutinized by inquisitors in Rome, who formed a department known as the Sacred Congregation of the Index, one of the Vatican readers considered the story of slavery in the United States to be a coded appeal for revolution. When a second opinion on the book was sought from other inquisitors, they did not consider it harmful and no ban was ever pronounced.

Prior to World War II, "Adolf Hitler's hate-filled *Mein Kampf* was also never put on the Index.... The censors pondered what to do about the Nazi dictator, with the discussions in the office going on for years." In the end, examination of *Mein Kampf* was simply terminated.

More recently, letters sent by Cardinal Joseph Ratzinger to a German literary critic discussed the Harry Potter novels. "In March 2003, a month after the English press throughout the world falsely proclaimed that Pope John Paul II approved of Harry Potter, the man who was to become his successor sent a letter to a Gabriele Kuby outlining his agreement with her opposition to J. K. Rowling's offerings" as "morally unhealthy reading" for children. On the issue of *Harry Potter and the Half-Blood*, "in a letter on March 7, 2003, Cardinal Ratzinger, thanked Kuby for her 'instructive' book (titled *Harry Potter: Good or Evil?*), in which Kuby stated the Potter books corrupted the hearts of the young, preventing them from developing a properly ordered sense of good and evil, thus harming their relationship with God while that relationship is still in its infancy. 'It is good, that you enlighten people about Harry Potter, because those are subtle seductions, which act unnoticed and by this deeply distort Christianity in the soul, before it can grow properly,' wrote Ratzinger.

"The letter also encouraged Kuby to send her book on Potter to a prelate who had quipped about Potter during a press briefing which led to the false press about the Vatican support of Potter. At a Vatican press conference to present a study document on the New Age in April 2003, . . . Fr. Peter Fleetwood made a positive comment on the Harry Potter books in response to a question from a reporter. This resulted in headlines such as POPE APPROVES POTTER (*Toronto Star*), POPE STICKS UP FOR POTTER BOOKS (*BBC Newsround*), and HARRY POTTER IS OKAY WITH THE PONTIFF (*Chicago Sun Times*)."

Largely because Dan Brown's *The Da Vinci Code* presented a tale of an investigation into a centuries-old conspiracy by the Church and Crusaders known as the Knights Templar to keep a secret about Jesus, that if revealed would shake the foundations of Christianity, nothing in the Vatican Secret Archives has been more fascinating to millions of people around the world than finding out what lies within the archives about the notorious knights.

CHAPTER 2

The Truth About the Templars

No pope has had a longer-lasting influence on the course of world history than Urban II. Today's conflict between Christianity-based democracies of the Western world and Middle East Islamic-fundamentalist terrorists can be traced to his appeal to Christian princes in Europe for a crusade to rescue the Holy Land from Muslims.

"In the speech given at the Council of Clermont in France, on November 27, 1095, he combined the ideas of making a pilgrimage to the Holy Land with that of waging a holy war.... He declared, 'The noble race of Franks (French) must come to the aid of their fellow Christians in the East. The infidel Turks are advancing into the heart of Eastern Christendom; Christians are being oppressed and attacked; churches and holy places are being defiled. Jerusalem is groaning under the Saracen (Muslim) yoke. The Holy Sepulchre [the church in Jerusalem that Christian tradition marks as the burial site of Christ] is in Moslem hands and has been turned into a mosque. Pilgrims are harassed and even prevented from access to the Holy Land. The West must march to the defense of the East. All should go, rich and poor alike. The Franks must stop their internal wars and squabbles. Let them go instead against the infidel and fight a righteous war. God himself will lead them, for they will be doing His work. There will be absolution and remission of sins for all who die in the service of Christ. Here they are poor and miserable sinners; there they will be rich and happy. Let none hesitate; they must march next summer. God wills it!' "

Between 1095 and 1250, there were seven crusades, but after initial success in capturing Jerusalem, the crusaders failed to hold the Holy Land. Out of these nearly two hundred years of military expeditions in the name of God by medieval warriors came such romantic figures as the real King Richard the Lionheart and the fictional knights of the round table of King Arthur's Camelot riding forth on a quest for the Holy Grail. But it was a twenty-first-century novel that lifted a group of Crusaders from history books to popular consciousness.

Of the Knights Templar, an eyewitness, Archbishop William of Tyre, wrote in 1118 that "certain noble men of knightly rank, religious men, devoted to God and fearing him, bound themselves to Christ's service" and promised to live "without possessions, under vows of chastity and obedience." Their leaders were Hugues de Payens, a knight of Burgundy, and Godefroid (Geoffrey) de St. Omer, from the south of France. Because they had "no church nor any fixed abode" when they arrived in Jerusalem, they were allowed "a dwelling place near the Lord's Temple" (the ruins of the Jewish temple in Jerusalem). Their primary duty was "protecting the roads and routes against the attacks of robbers and brigands." This they did, William of Tyre noted, "especially in order to safeguard pilgrims." For nine years following their founding, the Knights Templar wore secular clothing. They used "such garments as the people, for their soul's salvation, gave them."

Taking the name "Poor Knights of Christ and the Temple of Solomon," they became known as Templars. Sanctioned by the Church in 1128 at the Council of Troyes, they were soon renowned, and feared, for their ferocity in battle. "Following the retaking of Jerusalem by Islam in 1239, they obtained the island of Cyprus as their headquarters of the Order and used their vast accumulation of rich spoils of war to establish themselves as international financiers." Inventing banking, they set up a Temple in Paris, becoming the medieval equivalent of today's World Bank and World Trade Organization. Richer than any government on the continent, these former "Poor Knights of Christ" had evolved from nine members to between 15,000 and 20,000, with 9,000 manors and castles.

"They have now grown so great that there are in this Order today," William of Tyre wrote at some time between 1170 and 1174, "about 300 knights who wear white mantles, in addition to the brothers, who are almost countless. They are said to have immense possessions both here and overseas, so that there is now not a province in the Christian world which has not bestowed upon the aforesaid brothers a portion of its goods. It is said today that their wealth is equal to the treasures of kings."

The Templars had become so rich and powerful, William noted, they "have made themselves exceedingly troublesome."

Their leader at this time was Jacques de Molay. "Born in 1244 in Vitrey, France, he entered the Knights Templar in 1265 at the age of twenty-one. After rising quickly through the ranks, he spent a great deal of time in Great Britain. Eventually appointed as visitor general and grand preceptor of all England, he was made head of the order following the death of its twenty-second grand master. He then moved from England to Cyprus. It was there in the autumn of 1307 that he found himself called back to France by order of King Philip IV, known as 'the Fair,' and Pope Clement V. It is believed that the summons was the result of kingly and papal fear and envy of the power and wealth of the Templars. Another explanation is that Philip the Fair was so deep in debt to the Templars that he decided the only way to eradicate it was by eliminating the order.

"On Friday, October 13, 1307, royal bailiffs entered Templar headquarters in Paris and arrested the knights. Imprisoned and tortured, they were forced to confess to heresies, among them devil worship and sexual perversions. They were offered a choice of recantation or death. While de Molay gave a confession under torture, he quickly renounced it. Condemned along with another Templar, he was taken to an island in the Seine River in the shadow of Notre Dame Cathedral and set ablaze in 1312.

"A legend arose that as the flames raged around him, he prophesied that the king and pope would die within a year. The prophecy came true. But before his death the pope dissolved the order and warned that anyone even thinking about joining the Templars would be excommunicated and charged as heretics." Despite King Phillip and Pope Clement's decision to eradicate the Templars, some escaped their clutches and, it is believed, established the Order in Scotland. Today the Knights Templar survive as a component of Freemasonry.

Although the archives of the Vatican and volumes of European history contain numerous accounts of interlacing objectives of kings and popes, and even instances of conspiracies, none matched the deal between Pope Clement V and Phillip the Fair to cloak avarice in religion. That Clement recognized the illegitimacy of the charges of heresy against the Knights Templar was recorded in a document that was placed in the Vatican's secret archives and remained there for seven centuries.

To the astonishment of historians in 2008, the Vatican announced it would be publishing 799 copies of the minutes of the trials against the Templars, *Processus Contra Templarios* (*Papal Inquiry into the Trial of the Templars*) which it planned to sell for about $8,000 (5,900 euros, 4,115 British pounds). The giant work would come in a soft leather case, with detailed reproductions of the original Latin documents on the Templars trials.

Known as the Chinon parchment, for the location in France where the trials were held, the document recorded why Pope Clement V dissolved the Templars and issued arrest warrants for all members. The small parchment had been discovered in the Vatican's secret archives in 2001 by Professor Barbara Frale.

"I could not believe it when I found it," she said. "The paper was put in the wrong archive in the seventeenth century.

"The document…reveals that the Templars had an initiation ceremony which involved 'spitting on the cross,' 'denying Jesus,' and kissing the lower back, navel and mouth of the man proposing them for membership. The Templars explained to Pope Clement that the initiation mimicked the humiliation that knights could suffer if they fell into the hands of the Saracens, while the kissing ceremony was a sign of their total obedience. The Pope concluded that the ritual was not truly blasphemous, as alleged by King Philip when he had the knights arrested. However, he was forced to dissolve the Order to keep peace with the French and prevent a schism in the church.

"This is proof that the Templars were not heretics," said Professor Frale.

"The document contains the absolution Pope Clement V gave to the Grand Master of the Temple, Jacques de Molay, and to the other heads of the Order, after they 'had shown to be repented' and asked to be forgiven by the Church. After the formal abjuration, which is compelling for all those who were even only suspected of heretical crimes, the leading members of the Templar Order are reinstated in the Catholic Communion and readmitted to receive the sacraments. The document deals with the first phase of the trial of the Templars, when Pope Clement V was still convinced he might be able to guarantee the survival of the military-religious order and meet the apostolic need to remove the shame of excommunication from the warrior friars, caused by their previous denial of Jesus Christ when tortured by the French Inquisitor.

"As several contemporary sources confirm, the pope ascertained that Templars were involved in some serious forms of immorality and he planned a radical reform of the Order to subsequently merge it into one body with another military-religious order. . . . The Act of Chinon, a requirement to carry out the reform, remained however a dead letter. The French monarchy reacted by initiating a blackmail mechanism, which would have obliged Clement V to take a final decision during the Council of Vienna (1312). Unable to oppose the will of King, Phillip the Fair, who ordered the elimination of the Templars, the Pope heard the opinion of the Council Fathers and decided to abolish the Order. . . . Clement stated that this suffered decision did not amount to an act of heretic condemnation, which could not be reached on the basis of the various inquiries carried out in the years prior to the Council. . . .

"According to the pontiff, the scandal aroused by the 'shameful accusations' against the Knights Templar (heresy, idolatry, homosexuality and obscene behavior) would have dissuaded anyone from wearing the Templar habit and on the other hand, a delay on a decision regarding these issues would produce the squandering of the great wealth the Christians in the Holy Land offered to the Templars, charged with the duty to help fight against the enemies of the Faith in the Holy Land. The attentive consideration of these dangers, together with the pressure of the French, convinced the Pope to abolish the Order of the Knights of the Temple."

Pope Clement's absolution was of no earthly value to de Molay. For the sins and crimes against God and the Church to which he confessed under torture, he was burned at the stake. Other Templars were also executed, and the Templar treasures were confiscated by King Phillip.

Following publication of the Chinon document, the *London Daily Telegraph* reported "that the Association of the Sovereign Order of the Temple of Christ had launched a court case in Spain, demanding that Pope Benedict 'recognize' the seizure of Templar assets worth [100 billion euros]. The Spanish-based group of Templars declared, 'We are not trying to cause the economic collapse of the Roman Catholic Church, but to illustrate to the court the magnitude of the plot against our Order.'"

Of the revelations in the Chinon parchment *Time* magazine noted, "The notion of that much money, power and influence vanishing at a Papal pen stroke appears to have been too much for the mythic sensibility of the West, which wanted to believe that the Templars must somehow have survived, adapted, or been subsumed into another, even more secretive transnational group.

"Over the centuries, the allegedly still-extant order has been portrayed as malevolent, benign, heroic and occult. *Time* observed that "organizations all over the world, without any direct connection, have appropriated its name...Such homages should not obscure the fact that however much power they enjoy in the realm of fiction and fantasy, it almost certainly does not equal that which they once actually possessed—and then abruptly lost."

Five centuries after Pope Clement V colluded with Phillip the Fair to wipe out the Templars, the Vatican archives received a declaration known as a papal "bull" (encyclical) issued by Pope Leo XIII that prohibited membership by Catholics in the Freemasons. Titled *Humanum Genus*, issued on April 20, 1884, it stated, "Let no man think that he may for any reason whatsoever join the Masonic sect, if he values his Catholic name and his eternal salvation as he ought to value them." The Code of Canon Law, 1917 edition, in Canon 2335, declared, "Persons joining associations of the Masonic sect or any others of the same kind which plot against the

Church and legitimate civil authorities contract *ipso facto* excommunication simply reserved to the Apostolic See."

On July 18, 1974, Cardinal Franjo Šeper, Prefect of the Sacred Congregation for the Doctrine of the Faith, wrote a letter to the presidents of all the episcopal conferences, saying, "(1) the Holy See had repeatedly sought information from the bishops about contemporary Masonic activities directed against the Church; (2) there would be no new law on this matter, pending the revision of the Canon Law including Canon 2335, (3) all penal canons must be interpreted strictly, and (4) the express prohibition against Masonic membership by clerics, religious and members of secular institutes was to remain in force.'

"Many well-intentioned priests interpreted this letter ... as allowing lay Catholics to become Masons if the local bishop found that the lodge in question was not actively plotting against the Catholic Church or the civil authorities. Since Canon 2335 was in force at that time, and remained in force until 1983, they should have realized that even Cardinal Šeper had no authority to allow lay Catholics to become Masons. Cardinal Šeper, on February 17, 1981, attempted to end the confusion with a formal declaration [that said] his original letter did not in any way change the force of the existing Canon 2335, and the stated canonical penalties were in no way abrogated....

"When the new Code came out in 1983, Canon 1374 stated, 'A person who joins an association which plots against the Church is to be punished with a just penalty; one who promotes or takes office in such an association is to be punished with an interdict.'...

"Joseph Cardinal Ratzinger, then the new Prefect of the Congregation for the Doctrine of the Faith, and now Pope Benedict XVI, issued his *Declaration on Masonic Associations* ... [that] states 'the Church's negative judgment in regard to Masonic association remains unchanged since their principles have always been considered irreconcilable with the doctrine of the Church and therefore membership in them remains forbidden. The faithful who enrolled in Masonic associations would be in a state of grave sin and could not receive Holy Communion.'"

"The Vatican expected most copies of the Chinon parchment to be purchased by specialized libraries at top universities and by leading medieval scholars. The Livingston Masonic Library in New York may be the only Masonic-affiliated research facility to purchase a copy.... 'We are aware that this purchase will raise some eyebrows, both within and outside the Masonic fraternity,' noted Thomas M. Savini, director of the Livingston Masonic Library. 'But the acquisition of this work coincides with our mission to collect, study and preserve the Masonic heritage. The Masonic heritage includes investigation into Freemasonry's historical roots, but also the study of its inspirational roots, which include Rosicrucianism; the study of philosophy from the European Enlightenment; and study of the Knights Templar. This collection of documents is important not only to students of Freemasonry, but to medieval and religious scholars and historians as well. It is important that someone in the U.S. make this available, and the Library's Board of Directors unanimously agreed that it should be us.' "

CHAPTER 3

Vatican Treasures

Standing on the left bank of the Tiber River in Rome, adjacent to the ancient Circus of Nero, where tradition holds that "St. Peter, the first pope and the apostle to whom Christ entrusted his ministry, was martyred in A.D. 67. The seat of the Holy See and the pope's principal place of residence, it is the smallest independent state in the world." But is it the richest?

"In A.D. 320–27, the emperor Constantine built a five-aisled basilica" on what is believed to be the site of St. Peter's grave, "with a shrine in the apse of the church to mark the location of Peter's tomb. By the fifteenth century, the building was in disrepair and more space was needed, and plans were made to repair and expand the church." In the reign of Pope Julius II (1503–13), known as the Warrior Pope because he "donned armor to lead troops in defense of papal lands," work was commenced on a tomb for Julius, an enormous freestanding monument designed by Michelangelo. Julius then decided to tear down the Constantinian basilica and rebuild St. Peter's entirely.

"At the same time, Julius commissioned frescoes for the interior of the Vatican palace. He asked Raphael to paint four rooms for use as papal offices and reception spaces." While Raphael worked, Michelangelo was painting the ceiling of the papal chapel known as the Cappella Sistina, or Sistine Chapel (1508–12). "Michelangelo painted the vault with scenes from the book of Genesis: the Creation of the world and of Adam and

Eve, the Fall and Expulsion from the Garden of Eden, and God's destruction of the world by the flood. . . .

"In 1546, Michelangelo, now seventy-one years old, was named the architect of St. Peter's and dismantled some construction" and began work on "the first great dome to be raised on a colonnade. Designed by Michelangelo, but not completed until after his death, it crowns the church."

The geographical center of the Roman Catholic Church, the Vatican possesses many of the world's most precious works of art, and it is believed by many to be the world's wealthiest organization.

In a book on Vatican treasures, *The Vatican Billions*, Avro Manhattan noted, "The Catholic church is the biggest financial power, wealth accumulator and property owner in existence. She is a greater possessor of material riches than any other single institution, corporation, bank, giant trust, government or state of the whole globe. The pope, as the visible ruler of this immense amassment of wealth, is consequently the richest individual of the twentieth century. No one can realistically assess how much he is worth in terms of billions of dollars."

According to the author, the Holy See maintained large investments with the Rothschilds of Britain, France and America, the Hambros Bank, and Credit Suisse in London and Zurich. In the United States, it has holdings with the Morgan Bank, the Chase-Manhattan Bank, First National Bank of New York, the Bankers Trust Company, and others. Among its investments are billions of shares in the most powerful international corporations. such as Gulf Oil, Shell, General Motors, General Electric, IBM, and others. A conservative estimate set the amount of investments at more than $500 million in the United States alone.

In a recent statement published in connection with a bond prospectus, the Boston archdiocese listed its assets at $635,891,004, which was 9.9 times its liabilities. This left a net worth of $571,704,953. "It is not difficult to discover the truly astonishing wealth of the church," said Manhattan, "once we add the riches of the twenty-eight archdioceses and 122 dioceses of the U.S.A., some of which are even wealthier than that of Boston. Some idea of the real estate and other forms of wealth controlled by the Catholic Church may be gathered by the remark of a member of the New

York Catholic Conference, that his church 'probably ranks second only to the United States government in total annual purchase.' "

These statistics indicated that the Roman Catholic Church, once all its assets have been calculated, was the most formidable stockbroker in the world. The Holy See, independently of each successive pope, was increasingly orientated toward the United States. An article in *The Wall Street Journal* said that the Vatican's financial deals in the United States alone were so big that very often it sold or bought gold in lots of a million or more dollars at one time.

The Vatican's treasure of solid gold had been estimated by the *United Nations World Magazine* to amount to several billion dollars. A large bulk of this was stored in gold ingots with the U.S. Federal Reserve Bank, while banks in Switzerland and England held the rest. The wealth of the Vatican in the United States alone was greater than that of the five wealthiest giant corporations of the country.

But in 1987, *Fortune* magazine reported, "For all its splendor, the Vatican is nearly broke." The article noted, "Having survived barbarian invasions, persecutions, countless plagues, and occasional schisms, the papacy now faces a modern-day problem: a deep financial squeeze. The costs of the Vatican's growing bureaucracy far exceed its means."

In the previous year, the Holy See took in $57.3 million from sources as diverse as fees for ceremonies; income from publications, newspaper ads, and the sale of videocassettes; and modest investment earnings of $18 million. With investments of some $500 million, the Vatican commanded fewer financial resources than many U.S. universities.

In the spring of 2008, the Vatican reported that its accountants had recorded a loss in its annual accounts for the first time in four years. The report said the Holy See lost nearly ten million euros after investing in dollars before the U.S. currency fell sharply against the euro. "And the hole in the budget would have been even worse," said one source, "if the Church had not raised rents on its Rome properties, on which the Church does not pay property taxes to the Italian state."

Rent hikes reportedly caused controversy in Rome where it was alleged that the Church had threatened to evict tenants who didn't pay up. The loss was also attributed to poor performances by the Vatican's media operations, which included a newspaper and radio station. They lost approximately fifteen million euros in the pervious year. In 2007, the Vatican reported an overall income of 236.7 million euros, while expenses totaled 245.8 million euros.

Much of the Vatican's income comes from donations from church members around the world. American Catholics give about $80 million. Experts estimated that the Vatican's total wealth in 2008 was in excess of five billion euros ($5 billion).

Exactly how much wealth the Vatican has in banks and stock portfolios is a matter of debate, and the Holy See does not say. But money and investments do not constitute the total measure of the wealth of Vatican City. The Holy See owns the world's greatest collection of art treasures. In museums, public displays, private chambers, marble corridors, churches, chapels, and St. Peter's Basilica can be found paintings, frescoes, drawings, sculptures, and stained-glass windows created by the world's greatest artists through centuries from the years before Christ to today.

"The first collection of antiquities in the world was made by Popes Julius II, Leo X, Clement VII, Paul III, and Pius V. Among these were the Torso of Heracles, the Belvedere Apollo, and the Laocoön. Clement XIV's activity in collecting antiquities was continued by Pius VI with such great success that their combined collections...were united in one large museum...the Museo Pio-Clementino. It contains eleven separate rooms filled with celebrated antiquities."

"The founding of the Vatican Museums can be traced back to 1503 when the newly-elected Pope Julius II della Rovere, placed a statue of Apollo in the internal courtyard of the Belvedere Palace built by Innocent VIII.... Scores of artifacts were added throughout the centuries and the collections were eventually reorganized under Benedict XIV (1740–1758) and Pope Clement XIII (1758–1769). They founded the Apostolic Library Museums: the Sacred (Museo Sacro, 1756) and Profane (Museo Profano, 1767). The Christian Museum, comprising finds from the catacombs that could not be conserved in situ, was founded by Pius IX in 1854 in the Lateran Palace and was moved to the Vatican Museums by Pope John XXIII.

Pope Pius XI inaugurated in 1932...the Vatican Picture Gallery (the Pinacoteca)."

Much of the Vatican's collection of treasures is open to the public in its many museums and within the Vatican in the form of art and sculpture. The most famous and popular are the ceilings of the Sistine Chapel, painted by Michelangelo, and his sculpture, the *Pietà*, depicting the Virgin Mary holding his crucified body, on display in the Pietà Chapel in St. Peter's Basilica. Described by the Vatican as "probably the world's most famous sculpture of a religious subject, it was carved when Michelangelo was twenty-four years old, and it is the only one he ever signed.

"With this magnificent statue Michelangelo has given us a highly spiritual and Christian view of human suffering," noted a Vatican publication. "Artists before and after Michelangelo always depicted the Virgin with the dead Christ in her arms as grief stricken, almost on the verge of desperation. Michelangelo, on the other hand, created a highly supernatural feeling. As she holds Jesus's lifeless body on her lap, the Virgin's face emanates sweetness, serenity and a majestic acceptance of this immense sorrow, combined with her faith in the Redeemer. It seems almost as if Jesus is about to reawaken from a tranquil sleep and that after so much suffering and thorns, the rose of resurrection is about to bloom."

After St. Peter's Tomb, the Pietà Chapel is the most frequently visited and silent place in the entire basilica. The sculpture is protected by bulletproof glass to prevent a repeat of an attack upon it by a deranged man. In 1972, a thirty-three-year-old, Hungarian-born Australian, Laszlo Toth, leaped over a guardrail in St. Peter's crying, "I'm Jesus Christ!" and attacked the statue with a hammer. The left arm of the Virgin was shattered and the nose, left eye, and veil were chipped. The attack was the first major damage suffered by a work of art in St. Peter's since a German broke two fingers off the statue of a kneeling Pope Pius VI in 1970.

The museums of the Vatican are filled with artwork by Giotto, Caravaggio, Michelangelo, Leonardo da Vinci, and Raphael, among many others. The libraries of the Vatican hold ancient manuscripts of the Bible and other literature, in some cases the only copy of a certain work. The buildings of the Vatican, especially St. Peter's Basilica, are ornamented with gold, silver, precious stones, and the finest marble. "To understand why the Pope has such collections," explained the Vatican's expert in charge of maintaining them, Maurizio de Luca, "one must think about what the Church and the pope have meant over the centuries. The popes and their court at the time were the greatest supporters of culture. This is the place where the popes put some of the greatest artists to work and these have now become collections."

In 2001, "two former senior officials at the Vatican were charged in Rome in connection with an alleged art fraud. Monsignor Michele Basso, an ex-administrator of the chapter of St. Peter's, and Monsignor Mario Giordana, a former counselor in the Vatican's Italian embassy, were accused of trying to sell works of art falsely attributed to artists such as Michelangelo, Guercino and Giambologna, to art institutions such as the Metropolitan Museum in New York and the National Gallery in Washington.... The most remarkable works were a marble bust, the Young St. John the Baptist, attributed to Michelangelo, and an antique Greek vase attributed to Euphronius. The officials allegedly used headed Vatican notepaper to authenticate the works and enhance their value."

Because the Vatican is both a city and a state (both within the city of Rome), it runs in the same manner as governments, with a need to account for all its wealth, but it also operates like a worldwide corporation. Author Karl Keating recently noted that the Vatican's annual budget was about the size of that of the Archdiocese of Chicago. The funds went partly for the upkeep of the Vatican itself and partly for the Church's missionary and other work around the world.

"I suppose we could ask why the Vatican has trouble balancing its rather small annual budget," Keating wrote. "The wealth of the Church is almost entirely in church buildings, hospitals, schools, and missions, plus artworks. You could sell off the artworks, but the proceeds wouldn't feed the poor of the world for even a day.

"If the Vatican sold all its artworks, they would bring in hundreds of millions of dollars—but only once. Then they would be gone, and that money wouldn't go very far.... The popes are custodians, not owners.

They have a responsibility to preserve its artistic treasures for posterity, not to sell them off to private collections."

It has been calculated that "it costs about $250 million a year to operate the Vatican. The money comes from...contributions from bishops' conferences, dioceses, religious orders, individual lay donors, and 'other entities.' For 2004, that total came to $89 million. Of this amount, roughly $27.2 million came from individual dioceses under the terms of canon 1271 of the Code of Canon Law, which obligated dioceses to contribute to the financial support of the Holy See. This means that the 2,883 ecclesiastical jurisdictions in the world gave an average of $10,000 each in 2004....Wealthy archdioceses gave much more, a lot of smaller dioceses gave little or nothing."

The Vatican also garners "earnings on real estate, which refers principally to roughly 30 buildings and 1,700 apartments owned by the Holy See in Rome, which produced revenue of $64.5 million in 2004. Earnings [also come] from investments and other financial activities, with the Vatican's portfolio divided into 80 percent bonds and 20 percent stocks. In 2004, the Vatican's financial statement did not provide a comprehensive total," but experts said the "earnings must have been in the range of $100 million. The statement noted that this was an improvement of $21.5 million, attributed to an improved situation in the world financial markets in 2004."

"[A 2004] statement from the Vatican indicated that contributions to Peter's Pence, a fund to support papal charities that are not part of the regular Vatican budget, totaled $52 million,...a decline of 7.4 percent."

The best-selling author and Chicago priest, Father Andrew Greeley, wrote, "There was perhaps a time when the Church was truly rich (and that is another story), but the Reformation and the French Revolution ended that. Catholicism is property poor. What, for example, is the replacement value of St. Peter's [Basilica] in the Vatican? Who would buy it? How much income does it produce a year? In fact, the votive candle offerings—its only source of income—barely pay for maintenance. And what would someone do with it if they purchased it, especially once they discovered it was a loss leader? Build condos over it? What would one do with the Vatican museum? Maybe the Italian government could buy it as a station on the unfinished Roman metro line. The Vatican's endowment is less than that of a mid-level American Catholic university. It necessarily lives a hand-to-mouth financial existence. It puts on a great show with its splendors and its ceremonies, but the wealth that paid for its splendors vanished long ago and it can barely pay for the ceremonies."

"The Vatican's assets [have always been] a well-kept secret but one which is the topic of much speculation. Estimates range from $1.5 billion to $15 billion and more. They include works of art and buildings, which for the most part cannot be sold. Large parts of the Vatican's assets are in securities and gold reserves. Additional assets are in rental revenues, the sale of coins, stamps and souvenirs." Like palaces, royal residences, historic stately homes and manors in Great Britain, the Vatican has become a tourist attraction and money raiser.

Financial experts note that despite its wealth, the Vatican's budget has shown a deficit of several million dollars since 2001, but its debt is secured by assets. The largest include the Vatican's properties in and around Rome, the papacy's summer residence in Castel Gandolfo, office buildings, palaces and cathedrals. Vatican City, with fortress walls dating back to the sixteenth century, gained independent status in 1929 after the conclusion of "Lateran Pacts" with Italy. On February 11 of that year, Pope Pius XI and Benito Mussolini created the Vatican in its current dimensions and secured additional sovereignty rights and buildings.

According to Ivan Ruggiero, the Holy See's chief accountant, Vatican real estate is worth about $1.21 billion, not including its priceless art treasures. "The value of the real estate holding was calculated without taking into account its real value on the market," said Ruggiero. "And of course, the vast artistic holding of the Holy See was not taken into account, since it is a priceless and non-commercial holding. (Because of it being 'priceless,' the value of the art treasures has been listed as 'One Euro.')" St. Peter's Basilica is categorized "beyond market values."

In July 2008, the Associated Press reported that the Vatican ran a deficit in 2007, which the Holy See attributed to "the weak dollar in the

generous collection baskets from the U.S. faithful," and steep costs of running the Vatican's media (a newspaper and radio station). "The Vatican issued financial figures showing a nearly $13.5 million deficit. It cited the
sharp drop in the exchange rate for the U.S. dollar. The Vatican in Rome
pays many of its expenses in euros, a currency that had soared in value
against the U.S. dollar. The financial report, released by the Holy See's
press office, listed 2007 revenue of $371.97 million against expenses of
$386.27 million.

"The Vatican said its financial investments were hurt 'principally by
the sharp and rather marked inversion in exchange rates, above all for the
U.S. dollar.' The Vatican said rents and other income from its vast real estate holdings helped its finances. The Vatican Museums, which include
the Sistine Chapel, a top tourist attraction, also helped the Holy See's finances."

"The Vatican's annual Peter's Pence collection worldwide found that
the U.S. faithful were the most generous in absolute terms of the amount
donated, more than $18.7 million."

"No nation of Catholics gives more than Americans. A cardinals' advi-
sory committee on Holy See finances released a report in 2008 that showed
the U.S. was the top contributor nation ($19 million, or 29% of the total)
to the Holy See's charitable spending in 2007, and came in second (after
Germany) in contributions to the support of the Holy See itself."

In 2007, the Vatican decided to "give financial rewards to employees
who were doing a good job." "It said it would take into account employee
'dedication, professionalism, productivity and correctitude' when awarding a pay rise....More than 4,000 people, from cardinals to cleaners,"
were employed by the Holy See in the Vatican. "Base pay across a broad
spectrum of jobs reportedly ranged from 1,100 euros ($1,634) to 2,200
euros ($3,268) a month." A recent account gave the number of employees
at 2,659, of which 744 were diocesan priests, 351 men and women in religious orders, and 1,564 laity.

When Pope John XIII was asked how many people worked in the
Vatican, he quipped, "About half."

CHAPTER 4

Naughty Priests

W hen a Texas lawyer was digging in Vatican archives in 2003 in the pursuit of cases on behalf of American victims of sexual abuse by Catholic priests, he found a document titled *De Modo Provedendi di Causis Crimine Soliciciones (On the Manner of Proceeding in Cases of the Crime of Solicitation)*. Bearing the signature and seal of Pope John XXIII, it was written in 1962 by Cardinal Alfredo Ottaviani and distributed to senior clerics all over the world with an order that it was to be kept secret.

The sixty-nine-page document dealt primarily with any priest who tempted anyone in the act of sacramental confession "towards impure or obscene matters."

Bishops who received the order were instructed to pursue these cases "in the most secretive way." Everyone involved, including the alleged victim, was sworn "to observe the strictest secret, which is commonly regarded as a secret of the Holy Office" under penalty of excommunication. The "worst crime" was defined as "any obscene external deed, gravely sinful," carried out by a cleric "with a person of his own sex." The document was described as "strictly confidential" and was not to be published.

Seven centuries before Pope John XXIII authorized the Vatican's cover-up of sexual abuse of boys and young men by priests, St. Thomas Aquinas (1225–1274) stated "right reason declares the appointed end of sexual acts is procreation," and declared that homosexuality was one of the gravest of the *peccata contra naturam* or "sins against nature." But buried in Vatican archives are records of papal misbehavior that included Pope Clement VII having sex with page boys, Benedict IX engaging in both bestiality and bi-sexual orgies, and Boniface VII being described as a "monster" and a criminal. Leo I was a sadist and torturer, Julius III sodomized young boys, Clement VI frequented prostitutes, Anacletus raped nuns, and Paul II liked watching naked men being put on the rack and tortured.

Vatican archives and Church records attest to the problem of priestly sexual misbehavior, the Church's struggle to stamp it out, and instances of covering it up. One week after the election of the present Pope, Benedict XVI, in 2005, it was reported that in his previous position as head of the Congregation for the Doctrine of the Faith he had issued an order ensuring that investigations into sex abuse claims against priests be carried out in secret. It was alleged "in a confidential letter which was sent to every Catholic bishop in May 2001. It asserted the Church's right to hold inquiries behind closed doors and keep the evidence confidential for up to ten years after the victims reached adulthood. The letter was signed by Cardinal Joseph Ratzinger (the Pope's name before he was elected as John Paul II's successor).

"Lawyers acting for many abuse victims claimed that the letter was designed to prevent the allegations from becoming public knowledge or being investigated by the police. They accused Cardinal Ratzinger of committing a 'clear obstruction of justice.'

"The letter, 'concerning very grave sins,' was sent from the Congregation for the Doctrine of the Faith, the Vatican office that once presided over the Inquisition.... It spelled out to bishops the church's position on a number of matters ranging from celebrating the Eucharist with a non-Catholic to sexual abuse by a cleric 'with a minor below the age of eighteen years.' Ratzinger's letter stated that the church could claim jurisdiction in cases where abuse had been 'perpetrated with a minor by a cleric.' The letter stated that the church's jurisdiction 'begins to run from the day when the minor has completed the 18th year of age' and lasts for 10 years. It ordered that the 'preliminary investigations' into any claims of abuse should be sent to Ratzinger's office, which had the option of referring them back to private tribunals....

"Cases of this kind are subject to the pontifical secret," Ratzinger's letter concluded. Breaching the pontifical secret at any time while the 10-year jurisdiction order was operating carried penalties, including threat of excommunication.

"The letter was referred to in documents relating to a lawsuit filed earlier this year against a church in Texas and Ratzinger on behalf of two alleged abuse victims. By sending the letter, lawyers acting for the alleged victims claimed, the cardinal conspired to obstruct justice. Daniel Shea, the lawyer for the two alleged victims who discovered the letter, said: 'It speaks for itself. It's an obstruction of justice.'...

"Shea criticized the order that abuse allegations should be investigated only in secret tribunals. 'They are imposing procedures and secrecy on these cases. If law enforcement agencies find out about the case, they can deal with it. But you can't investigate a case if you never find out about it. If you can manage to keep it secret for 18 years plus 10 the priest will get away with it,' Shea added."

When Pope Benedict XVI made his first visit to the United States in April 2008, he told reporters on his plane on the way to Washington, DC, that the sexual abuse of children "is a great suffering for the church in the United States and for the church in general and for me personally that this could happen." He said, "As I read the histories of those victims, it is difficult for me to understand how it was possible that priests betrayed in this way. Their mission was to give healing, to give the love of God to these children. We are deeply ashamed and we will do what is possible that this cannot happen in the future."

Drawing a distinction between priests with homosexual tendencies and those inclined to molest children, the pontiff said, "I would not speak at this moment about homosexuality, but pedophilia, which is another thing. And we would absolutely exclude pedophiles from the sacred ministry."

Asserting that anyone guilty of pedophilia "cannot be a priest," he said that church officials were going through the seminaries that train would-be priests to make sure that those candidates have no such tendencies.

"We'll do all that is possible to have a strong discernment, because it is more important to have good priests than to have many priests," he said. "We hope that we can do, and we have done and will do in the future, all that is possible to heal this wound."

The Vatican archives and the annals of Christianity going back almost two thousand years contain accounts of the struggle with sexual misdeeds. In the year A.D. 390, Emperor Valentinian II was strongly influenced by his Christian beliefs when he decreed that men committing sodomy "shall expiate a crime of this kind in avenging flames in the sight of the people." In eighth-century England, a book that referred to sexual crimes committed by clerics against children, the *Penitential Bede*, advised that clerics who committed sodomy with children be given severe penalties, depending on their rank. In A.D. 1179, a Church council decreed that clerics who had committed "sins against nature" be confined to a monastery for life or be forced to leave the Church. In the sixteenth century, Pope Pius IV issued the first papal decree condemning solicitation of sex by priests. The next major statement of Church law, Sacramentum Poenitentiae, issued on June 1, 1741, by Pope Benedict XIV, decreed that all attempts by priests to lead congregants into sex be condemned. In 1917, a code was promulgated containing language condemning solicitation. Legislation on the subject of sexual solicitation was issued again in 1922.

At the time of the discovery of Pope John XXIII's 1962 secrecy edict in 2003, *The New York Times* News Service reported, "The sex-abuse crisis that engulfed the Roman Catholic Church during the past twelve months has spread to nearly every American diocese and involves more than 1,200 priests, most of whose careers span a mix of church history and seminary training. These priests are known to have abused more than 4,000 minors over the past six decades, according to an extensive *New York Times* survey of documented cases of sexual abuse by priests through Dec. 31, 2002. The survey, the most complete compilation of data on the problem available, contains the names and histories of 1,205 accused priests. It counted 4,268 people who claimed publicly or in lawsuits to have been abused by priests, though experts say there are surely many more who have remained silent. But the data show that priests secretly violated vulnerable youth long before the first victims sued the church and went public in 1984 in Louisiana. Some offenses date from the 1930s."

According to Los Angeles Police Department Complaint # BC307934, filed December 17, 2003, from 1955 through 2002 at least twenty-eight priests within the LA Archdiocese inner circle accused or convicted of sex abuse, "occupied the highest positions." The complaint stated, "Well placed priests including Bishops Juan Arzube and G. Patrick Ziemann 'used their prominence in the archdiocese administration to cover up for other priests. Priests involved in education such as Leland Boyer and Gerald Fessard utilized their positions of authority to gain access to victims and then to funnel the children they molested into seminaries and the priesthood. These twenty-six priests and likely many others occupied positions such as Auxiliary Bishops, Vicar for Clergy, Vicars General, deans, and teachers at local seminaries and as recruiters for seminaries. The elevation of child molesters to these positions helps explain why so many child-molesting priests were protected by the Defendant Doe Archdiocese, how so many child molesters became priests, and how so many seminarians and priests became child molesters."

Jeffrey Anderson, a Minnesota attorney who specialized in sexual abuse civil suits, was aware of more than three hundred civil claims against Catholic priests in forty-three states through 1991, and had handled eighty cases himself. Catholic reporter Jason Berry had tracked at least one hundred civil settlements by the Catholic Church in the years 1984–90, totaling $100 million to $300 million. Roman Catholic canon attorney Father Thomas Doyle estimated that about 3,000 Roman Catholic priests had been pedophiliac abusers of children (an average of sixteen priestly sex abusers per diocese).

Baltimore psychotherapist and former priest A. W. Richard Sipe, author of *A Secret World: Sexuality and the Search for Celibacy*, made a comprehensive study of the sexual conduct of priests. He reported, "Estimated chances that a Catholic priest in the United States is sexually active: one in two." Sipe studied 1,000 priests and 500 of their "'lovers' or victims." He found that "20 percent of priests were involved in sexual relationships with women, 8 to 10 percent in 'heterosexual exploration,' 20 percent were homosexual with half of them active, 6 percent were pedophiles, almost 4 percent of them targeted boys."

Offices of the national monthly *Freethought Today* in Madison, Wisconsin, reported receiving three to four newspaper clippings per week from readers detailing a new criminal or civil court accusation against a priest or Protestant minister. It had surveyed reported cases in North America during the years of 1988 and 1989 and found 250 reported cases of criminal charges involving child-molesting priests, ministers, or ministerial staff in the United States and Canada. Of the accused clergy, seventy were Catholic priests (39.5%) and 111 were Protestant ministers (58%).

Although priests made up only about 10 percent of North American clergy, they were 40 percent of the accused. With outcome unknown in about a fifth of the cases, the study found that "88 percent of all charged clergy were convicted (81 percent of priests were convicted)....A majority of the cases did not go to trial....Three quarters of all clergy who pleaded innocent were found guilty. About half of the Catholic priests pleading innocent were convicted."

The study revealed that Catholic priests were acquitted or dismissed of child molestation charges at a higher rate than Protestant ministers. Similarly, Catholic priests received a higher rate of suspended sentences when convicted, and when sentenced, spent considerably less time in jail or prison.

Angela Bonavoglia, author of the book *Good Catholic Girls: How Women Are Leading the Fight to Change the Church*, noted that many Catholic priests around the world—in Mexico, Latin America, Africa, and the United States—were involved in consensual relationships with women. Many other priests were involved in consensual relationships with adult men. "It is obvious that the crisis in the Church is much larger than pedophilia or the sexual abuse of minors," she wrote. "It is about crimes and criminals, sex and power, yes. But fundamentally, it is about hypocrisy. By forbidding priests who choose to be sexual in mature ways that include commitment, responsibility and respect, and by protecting them from the costs of their sexual exploits, the Church has effectively condoned a clerical sexual free-for-all. That heterosexual and homosexual behavior may thrive in the

Catholic priesthood does not reflect anything inherent about homo-sexuality or heterosexuality but is rather an indictment of the hypocrisy and duplicity of an elite, closed, all-male system, a secret society of sorts that condones, indeed, demands, lying about the reality of one's sexual life at all costs."

Asserting that Pope John XXIII's 1962 document remained in force until May 2001, the authors of the book *Sex, Priests, and Secret Codes* by Thomas P. Doyle, A. W. R. Sipe, and Patrick J. Wall, presented their account of what they called the Catholic Church's 2000-year paper trail of sexual abuse. They wrote that the letter was "significant" because it re-flected the Church's "insistence on maintaining the highest degree of se-crecy."

Forty-six years after Pope John XXIII signed *De Modo Provedendi di Causis Crimine Soliciciones* and pledged the Church to secrecy about sex abuse of youths by the clergy, Pope Benedict XVI in his tour of the United States and in Australia apologized privately to individuals who were abused by priests and frequently spoke publicly on the subject. To a World Youth Day audience in Sydney, Australia, he declared, "These mis-deeds, which constitute so grave a betrayal of trust, deserve unequivocal condemnation. They have caused great pain and have damaged the Church's witness. I ask all of you to support and assist your bishops, and to work together with them in combating this evil. Victims should receive compassion and care, and those responsible for these evils must be brought to justice. It is an urgent priority to promote a safer and more wholesome environment, especially for young people."

CHAPTER 5

Murder in Holy Orders

The archives of the Vatican contain evidence that being pope has been one of history's most dangerous jobs. Through the centuries many have been murdered or assassinated. The first was Pope John VIII. In 882, he was poisoned and then clubbed to death by scheming members of the papal court. According to Matthew Brunson's *The Pope Encyclopedia: An A to Z of the Holy See* most murders of pontiffs occurred in the Middle Ages, especially in a period described by Cardinal Cesare Baronius in *Annales ecclesiastici* as "the Iron Age of the Papacy," from 867 to 964, when powerful families had popes elected, deposed, and murdered to advance political ambitions, or as vengeance. Of the twenty-six popes during this era, sixteen died by violence.

The most tantalizing of the murders was that of John XII (955–964). "Just 18 years old when he was elected pontiff, John was a notorious womanizer and the papal palace came to be described as a brothel during his reign. He died of injuries after he was caught in bed by the husband of one of his mistresses. Some legends say that he died of a stroke while in the act of love."

Theories and claims of murderous cabals blossomed following the death of Pope Clement XIV in 1771. He "was reportedly so racked with guilt over disbanding the Jesuits that he spent his last years terrified of being poisoned." Following his death, there were so many stories about his possible murder that a postmortem was conducted. It found nothing to implicate the Jesuits.

The following is a list of murdered pontiffs and the manner in which they are thought to have been removed from *The Pope Encyclopedia*:

John VIII (872–882): Poisoned and clubbed to death
Adrian III, St. (884–885): Rumored poisoned
Stephen VI (896–897): Strangled
Leo V (903): Murdered
John X (914–928): Suffocated under a pillow
Stephen VII (VIII) (928–931): Possibly murdered
Stephen VIII (IX) (939–942): Mutilated and died from injuries
John XII (955–964): [Killed while caught in the act with a mistress by
    the woman's outraged husband] or suffered a stroke while with a
    mistress or murdered by an outraged husband
Benedict VI (973–974): Strangled by a priest
John XIV (983–984): Starved to death or poisoned
Gregory V (996–999): Rumored to have been poisoned
Sergius IV (1009–1012): Possibly murdered
Clement II (1046–1047): Rumored poisoned
Damasus II (1048): Rumored murdered
Boniface VIII (1294–1303): Died from abuse while a French captive

The most bizarre story of a pope is that of Stephen VII. In "896, [he] set in motion the trial of his rival, who had been dead for 9 months." Author Mark Owen noted in an article on the notorious pontiffs that the body of Pope Formosus was dragged from its tomb and placed on a throne. Wrapped in a hair shirt, the corpse was provided with legal counsel, who remained silent while Pope Stephen raved and screamed.

"The crime of Formosus," Owen recorded, "was that he had crowned emperor one of the numerous illegitimate heirs of Charlemagne after first having performed the same office for a candidate favored by Stephen.

"After Stephen's rant, the corpse was stripped of its clothes and its fingers were chopped off. It was then dragged through the palace and hurled from a balcony to a howling mob below, who threw it into the Tiber

River. The body was rescued by people sympathetic to Formosus and given a quiet burial. Stephen was strangled a few years later.

"In 964 Pope Benedict V raped a young girl and absconded to Constantinople with the papal treasury, only to reappear when the money ran out." A church historian called Benedict "the most iniquitous of all the monsters of ungodliness." He was also "slain by a jealous husband. His corpse, bearing a hundred dagger wounds, was dragged through the streets before being tossed into a cesspit. . . .

"In October 1032, the papal miter was purchased for eleven-year-old Benedict IX. Upon reaching his 14th year, a chronicler wrote that Benedict had surpassed in wantonness and profligacy all who had preceded him."

According to historian Peter de Rosa in his book *Vicars of Christ*, popes had mistresses as young as fifteen years of age, were guilty of incest and perversions of every sort, had innumerable children, [and] "were murdered in the very act of adultery."

Pope Alexander VI (formerly Rodrigo Borgia) reigned from 1492–1503. He committed his first murder at the age of twelve. "Upon assuming the Papal miter, he cried, 'I am Pope, Vicar of Christ!' Like his predecessor, Innocent VIII, Alexander sired many children, baptized them personally, and officiated at their weddings in the Vatican. He had ten known illegitimate children (including the notorious Cesare and Lucrezia Borgia), by his favorite mistress Vannoza Catanei. When she faded in allure, Borgia took fifteen-year-old Giulia Farnese. Farnese obtained a Cardinal's red hat for her brother, who later became Paul III. Alexander was followed by Julius II who purchased the papacy with his own private fortune. . . . A notorious womanizer, Julius was so eaten away with syphilis that he couldn't expose his foot to be kissed."

"Pope Sixtus IV charged Roman brothels a Church tax. According to historian Will Durant, in 1490 there were 6,800 registered prostitutes in Rome. Pope Pius II declared that Rome was the only city run by . . . the sons of popes and cardinals.

Pope Leo I (440–461) asserted that it did not matter how immoral or inept a pope was as long as he was deemed the rightful successor to St. Peter." There is no official list of popes, but the *Annuario Pontificio* [Papal

Yearbook], published every year by the Vatican, contains a list that is generally considered the most authoritative. It cites Benedict XVI as the 265th pope of Rome.

Number 263, John Paul I, received the designation on August 26, 1978. The first pontiff to choose two names (in honor of his predecessors, John XXIII and Paul VI), he was born Albino Luciani on October 17, 1912, in Forno di Canale (now called Canale d'Agordo), Italy. He differed from his predecessors in having never held a major position in the Vatican's internal government or diplomatic corps. Despite being prominent within Italy, he was largely unknown to the wider world.

Ordained on July 7, 1935, "he studied at Rome's Gregorian University before a brief period as curate in his childhood parish. After he was appointed to a deputy position at Belluno seminary in 1937, he spent years teaching, during which time he became vicar-general to the Bishop at Belluno. Toward the end of 1958, Pope John XXIII appointed Luciani as bishop of Vittorio Veneto, and after a slow start at the Vatican Council (1962–65), he soon became an active voice in doctrinal matters." Named archbishop of Venice (1969) and a cardinal in 1973, he rejected many of Catholicism's more opulent aspects and encouraged richer churches to give to poorer ones.

After his election to the papacy by the College of Cardinals, *Time* magazine reported, "The Cardinals knew what they wanted: a warm and humble man. Seated at a table in front of the Sistine Chapel altar, the Cardinal solemnly intoned the name written on each ballot. 'Luciani... Luciani...Luciani...' Beside him sat two other Cardinal scrutatores (vote counters) who carefully plucked the ballots from a silver chalice, unfolded them and passed them to their colleague. It was the fourth and final ballot of the astonishing one-day conclave that gave the Catholic world its 263rd Pope."

Succeeding in penetrating "the wall of secrecy that attends such conclaves, and the vows of silence taken by the Cardinals as they enter and are sealed from the outside world, *Time*'s reporters Jordan Bonfante and Roland Flamini pieced together much of the story of the proceedings in the Sistine Chapel. It was clear that Luciani came to power through no accident, but as a result of a spontaneous consensus that evolved from three agreements reached in a lengthy pre-conclave period that followed the death of Pope Paul VI on Aug. 6 [1978].

"Probably half of the 111 Cardinal-electors went into the conclave undecided. Most were fairly convinced that the Pope would have to be an Italian....

"The second consensus, resisted to the end by some members of the Curia, was that the Church, whatever its far-flung political and administrative problems, needed a pastoral Pope. 'It is one thing to interpret the faith and another to convey it to the people in the parishes,' said one ranking Curia prelate. 'That is something that the bishops—whatever their theology—understand better than the Curialists at their little desks.' "

Another Cardinal said, "I think all of us had agreed in our own minds before the conclave that we needed to go back to a humble, pastoral man, although we did not really consult each other about it. And then, when we went in, it became clear to us that this was what we wanted."

One participant said there was a consensus that the new Pope be "not obvious, and not controversial."

As the balloting produced no obvious leading candidate, Luciani was a man "not actively disliked by anyone, and actively liked by everyone who really knew him."

"At noon," the *Time* reporters wrote, "the two sets of ballots, skewered on a long needle and strung like a kind of combined ecclesiastical shish kebab and necklace, were thrust into the chapel stove along with black chemical flares to send up a dark 'no Pope' signal to the waiting crowds in St. Peter's Square. But the flue above the stove was broken, and black smoke seeped through the chapel, partially obscuring Michelangelo's famous frescoes. For a quarter of an hour, the assembled Cardinals coughed, covered their mouths and rubbed their eyes until two windows were opened to clear the air.

"As the Cardinals broke for lunch, walking to the Pontifical Hall in the palace's Borgia apartments, intense discussions were under way. On the third ballot, at 4:30...Luciani burst to the fore, falling just short of a majority.

"At that point," Luciani explained later with a grin that would earn him the nickname "the smiling pope," the situation "began to get dangerous for me."

"Cardinals Willebrands of the Netherlands and Ribeiro of Portugal, sitting on either side of him, leaned toward him. Whispered one: 'Courage. If the Lord gives a burden, he also gives the strength to carry it.' Whispered the other: 'The whole world prays for the new Pope.'"

On the fourth vote, "no other name but Luciani's was read out. There were a number of blank ballots.... But roughly ninety votes went to Luciani." Ringing applause echoed in the chapel. "The chapel door was opened and eight conclave aides entered to accompany Jean Cardinal Villot, the church's 'Camerlengo,' or chamberlain, to the flustered Luciani, who was still seated in his place under a fresco of the baptism of Christ. The Camerlengo, his face wreathed in smiles, asked the ritual question, 'Do you accept your canonical election as Supreme Pontiff?'

"Luciani at first replied, 'May God forgive you for what you have done in my regard.' Then he gave his assent, 'Accepto.'"

Burning ballots and chemically treated straw in a stove sent a puff of white smoke up a chimney, signaling to a throng in St. Peter's Square that the Church had a new pope. Inside, Luciani announced the name he had chosen for himself as the new pope. He would be "Ioannes Paulus." The crowd outside was told the name of their new pope was "John Paul."

"After the singing of the 'Te Deum' of thanksgiving, the pontiff was escorted to the sacristy to don his temporary papal robes. He reappeared in a white cassock with a shoulder-length cape and a high white sash. Grinning happily, he took the throne that had been erected in front of the altar, and joyful Cardinals approached one by one to embrace him and to kiss the papal ring."

"Rome did not get its first real look at John Paul until the next day, when 200,000 people filled St. Peter's Square for the weekly Sunday noon blessing. John Paul spoke for seven minutes.... Let us 'understand each other,' he told the crowd. 'I do not have the wisdom of heart of Pope John, nor the preparation and culture of Pope Paul. However, now I am in their place and must try to help the church. I hope you will help me with your prayers.'...

"The new pope, John Paul, gave a glimpse of his personal style with the plans for his Sept. 3 open-air accession ceremonies. At his direction it was not called a 'coronation' or 'enthronement,' but a 'solemn Mass to mark the start of his ministry as Supreme Pastor.' John Paul asked not to be carried on the usual portable throne but to walk in procession. Most significant, he did not wish to be crowned with the triple-decked, bee hive-shaped tiara. Instead, a pallium, the white woolen stole symbolizing his title of Patriarch of the West, would be placed on his shoulders. . . .

"In his inaugural address to the Cardinals, John Paul pledged to carry forward the work of the Second Vatican Council, convened by Pope John XXIII in 1962 and concluded by Paul VI in 1965. He would, he said, put a 'priority' on a revision of the canon law codes." It was immediately recognized that John Paul intended "a new style of papacy, more simple and less formal than many at the Vatican were used to. His first speech to the world, delivered from the balcony of St. Peter's Basilica, was personal and direct. . . . He asked Catholics to 'have mercy on the poor new pope who never really expected to rise to this post.' He joked about having to pick up the Vatican's thick yearbook, the *Annuario Pontificio*, to study how the Roman Curia worked."

"The new pope made no secret of the fact that he felt a bit intimidated by the church structure he was supposed to be running. . . . In public events he made connections with everyday Catholics by adopting a storytelling manner of preaching and bringing a parish atmosphere to the Vatican. He explained the concept of free will with a metaphor about prudent automobile maintenance. He spoke sympathetically about those who could not bring themselves to believe in God. He jokingly compared marriage to a gilded birdcage. 'Those on the outside are dying to get in,' he said, 'while those on the inside are dying to get out.'"

He shocked many Catholics by saying that God "is a father, but even more, a mother'" in the way He loves humanity. He quoted the Old Testament prophet Isaiah: "Could a mother forget her child? But even if that were to happen, God will never forget his people."

Some church commentators viewed his "pontificate as a time of grace and joy," calling him "the smiling pope." "Other analysts characterized

Pope John Paul as out of his depth, and as a man who was overwhelmed by the burdens of his new position." Vatican veterans and traditionalists worried that John Paul was too liberal and feared that he intended to revolutionize Church doctrines, including revising laws on contraception.

Cardinal Ratzinger saw "great goodness, simplicity, humanity and courage."

In an article by Ruth Bertels, she writes that on the evening of September 28, 1978, when John Paul "sat down for dinner in the third-floor dining room of the Apostolic Palace, his two secretaries, Father Diego Lorenzi, who had worked closely with him in Venice for more than two years, and Father John Magee, newly appointed since the papal election, were present. Nuns had prepared a simple supper of clear soup, veal, fresh beans, and a salad." The three men ate while watching the news on television." The Pope appeared in good spirits and good health.

"On the floor below, lights were still on at the Vatican Bank, where its head, Bishop Paul Marcinkus, [had recently received a report about the Pope's] investigation of the Vatican Bank and the bishop's methods of running it, including its recent takeover of the Banca Cattolica." Its shares were held by various dioceses, but the majority rested with the Vatican Bank.

"Cardinal Jean Villot, the Vatican secretary of state, was also still at his desk that evening studying the changes the pope had given him an hour before. Villot had pleaded and argued..., but the pope was adamant. The changes would stand."

In Buenos Aires, banker Roberto Calvi and a pair of associates, Licio Gelli and Umberto Ortolani, knew that "the Bank of Italy had been secretly investigating Calvi's Milan bank since April, prompted by a public campaign against Calvi, begun in 1977, giving details of criminal activities....

"In New York, Sicilian banker Michele Sindona had been fighting the Italian government's effort to extradite him to Milan to face charges involving a fraudulent diversion of $225 million. A federal judge had ruled in May that the extradition should be granted. While free on a 3 million dollar bail, Sindona had demanded that the United States government prove that there was well-founded evidence to justify the extradition. The hearing was scheduled for November."

In Chicago, Cardinal John Cody, "head of an archdiocese of "2½ million, with nearly 3,000 priests, 450 parishes, and an annual income he refused to" disclose knew that numerous organizations had petitioned Rome to remove him.

The pope went to bed. Nighttime quiet enveloped the Vatican.

In the predawn hours of September 29, 1978, the Pope's housekeeper knocked at his bedroom door, as she always did, promptly at 4:30 A.M. Hearing no response, she left. "She returned fifteen minutes later to find him still not stirring." When she entered his bedroom, "she found him propped up in bed, still holding his papers from the night before." Dead.

"On the night table beside him lay an opened bottle of Effortil, a medication for his low blood pressure." The shaken and tearful housekeeper immediately informed the papal chamberlain, Cardinal Villot. Villot arrived in the Pope's room at 5:00 A.M. and gathered the crucial papers, the Effortil bottle, and several personal items that were soiled with vomit. None of these items were seen again.

"The Vatican claimed that its house physician had determined myocardial infarction as the cause of death. Although Italian law required a waiting period of at least 24 hours before a body may be embalmed, Cardinal Villot had the body of Albino Luciani prepared for burial 12 hours after his death. Although the Vatican refused to permit an autopsy on the basis of ... canon law, the Italian press verified that an autopsy had been" done on Pope Pius VIII in 1830.

The initial report to the public was that "the Holy Father was found dead by Sister Vincenzia and not by his secretary.... One report had him dead in his bathroom, another by his desk in his bedroom." There were also discrepancies about the time of death, though the official estimate was that he died at 11 P.M. on September 28.

"Another report stated John Paul had complained during the day of feeling sick but wouldn't call a doctor. It said he had suffered a pain and a violent cough during that afternoon." It was reported that "after dinner he rushed down the hallway to get a telephone call around 9:15 pm."

Did this trigger a fatal heart attack? Or had he been poisoned?

Some who believed he was murdered stated that the motive was fear that the spiritual leader of Roman Catholics was embarking on a revolution. He wanted to set the Church in a new direction that was considered undesirable and dangerous by many of the high-ranking Church officials.

In a 1984 book titled *In God's Name: An Investigation into the Murder of John Paul I*, British author David Yallop contended that the pontiff was ordered killed by one or more of six suspects, all of whom "had a great deal to fear if the papacy of John Paul I continued." Among those in the Vatican with a reason to worry were numerous members of a clandestine Italian Masonic lodge called Propaganda Due [doo-ay], or P2. Founded in 1877, in Turin, as "Propaganda Massonica," it had as members politicians and government officials from across Italy. "The name was changed to 'Propaganda Due' following World War II when the Grand Orient numbered its lodges." Although the Church banned Catholics from joining the Freemasons, P2 extended its reach into the Holy See in the form of "The Great Vatican Lodge." In September 1978, members included cardinals, bishops, many high-ranking prelates, and laymen.

The Grand Master was Licio Gelli. A financier, he had been a Mussolini fascist, "liaison officer" for the Nazis, organizer of a "rat line" to assist Nazis in avoiding arrest as war criminals by fleeing to Argentina, ally of Argentine dictator Juan Peron, post–World War II informant for both U.S. Intelligence and Italian Communists, and agitator for the establishment of a right-wing government in Italy.

According to Yallop, the murder of John Paul was triggered by his decision to purge the troubled Vatican Bank and cleanse the Church of ties to P2.

"The man who had quickly been labeled 'The Smiling Pope,'" wrote Yallop, "intended to remove the smiles from a number of faces the following day."

Yallop cited Villot, who had learned he would be replaced as the Vatican's Secretary of State and who was dismayed that John Paul was thinking of loosening the church's prohibition on artificial birth control;

Marcinkus, head of the Vatican Bank, who was said to have been scheduled for immediate removal; Roberto Calvi, president of Banco Ambrosiano, who faced ruin if his trickery with Vatican funds were discovered; Sindona, who knew about the Vatican Bank's alleged laundering of Mafia money; Gelli; and John Cardinal Cody of Chicago, who was said to have been tipped off that he would be asked to resign.

Yallop speculated that the Pope was poisoned, possibly by someone tampering with a bottle of low blood pressure medicine called Effortil that John Paul was said to have kept at his bedside. Yallop wrote that these inconsistencies in the Vatican's account of the papal death and the absence of an autopsy pointed to a cover-up.

"It was abundantly clear," he wrote, "that on September 28th, 1978, these six men, Marcinkus, Villot, Calvi, Sindona, Cody and Gelli had much to fear if the Papacy of John Paul I continued. It is equally clear that all of them stood to gain in a variety of ways if Pope John Paul I should suddenly die."

Conspiracy theorists were quick to find a prediction of John Paul's murder in the writings of the ancient prophet Nostradamus:

> The one elected Pope will be mocked by his electors,
> This enterprising and prudent person will suddenly be reduced in silence,
> They cause him to die because of his too great goodness and mildness.
> Stricken by fear, they will lead him to his death in the night.

All that could be said with certainty was that John Paul had been Pope for thirty-three days

EVENTS AFTER JOHN PAUL'S DEATH:

October 1978: Election of Polish Cardinal Karol Wojtyła to the papacy. He takes the name John Paul II in honor of the dead Pope. None of John Paul I's instructions or edicts are carried out.

January 21, 1979: Judge Emillio Alessandrini, a magistrate investigating the Banco Ambrosiano activities is murdered.

March 20, 1979: Nino Pecorelli, an investigative journalist, exposing membership and dealings of the Freemason's P-2 group, is murdered.

July 11, 1979: Giorgio Ambrosioli, following his testimony concerning Sindona and Calvi in Vatican business circles, is murdered.

July 13, 1978: Lt. Col. Antonio Varisco, head of Rome's security service, is murdered. Varisco was also investigating the activities of the P-2 group; he was seen speaking with Giorgio Ambrosioli two days before Ambrosioli's death.

February 2, 1980: The Vatican withdraws an agreement to provide videotaped depositions of Sindona in his trial in the U.S. on charges of fraud, conspiracy and misappropriation of funds in connection with the collapse of Franklin National Bank.

May 13, 1980: Sindona attempts suicide.

July 8, 1980: Roberto Calvi, also jailed for fraud, attempts suicide.

September 1, 1981: The Vatican Bank acknowledges its controlling interests in a number of banks fronted by Calvi—for more than one billion dollars of debt.

January 2, 1981: Shareholders in Banco Ambrosiano send a letter to John Paul II that expose the connections between the Vatican Bank and Roberto Calvi, P-2 and the Mafia. The letter is never acknowledged.

April 27, 1982: Attempted murder of Roberto Rosone, General Manager of Banco Ambrosiano. Rosone was reportedly trying to clean up the bank's operations.

October 2, 1982: Giuseppe Dellacha, executive of Banco Ambrosiano, dies after a fall out of one of the bank's windows.

March 23, 1986: Michele Sindona, in the Italian jail for which he was serving time for ordering the death of Giorgio Ambrosioli, is poisoned to death.

The most sensational of these events occurred on June 17, 1982. On that date, Roberto Calvi was found hanging by the neck from a bridge in London.

CHAPTER 6

The Mystery of the Pope's
Banker

On June 21, 1982, a postal clerk on his way to work in London glanced over "the parapet of the embankment of Blackfriars Bridge and noticed orange nylon rope lashed to a scaffolding pole under the bridge." Hanging from it was the body of a man, "suavely dressed in his own topcoat and expensive Patek Philippe watch on his wrist, loafers by the same firm were on his feet....In his wallet were about 10,000 pounds sterling, Swiss francs and Italian lira. Stuffed into the pockets and down his flies were bricks and stones that the police believed came from a nearby building site.

"The presence of the money and the watch appeared to rule out a mercenary murder. At the same time, a coroner found no marks on Calvi's body indicating he had [not] been the object of violence before his death, no syringe marks to suggest he had been drugged, and no drugs in his system besides the residue of the single sleeping pill he had taken the night before." A coroner's jury filed a verdict of suicide.

Because this ruling made no sense to Calvi's widow, son and daughter, "they challenged the original inquest. A second one, held in London in 1983,...[ruled] it was impossible to say whether Calvi had killed himself or been killed by others. Yet Carlo Calvi, the banker's only son, who was studying for a doctorate at Washington's Georgetown University when his father died, refused to give in...So in 1989 he hired a firm of private detectives to take the forensic investigation further than had the London Police.

"Kroll Associates located the scaffolding poles from which Calvi had been suspended, reassembled them exactly as they had been under Blackfriars Bridge, and then had a stand-in for Calvi, of the same height and weight, take the route that Calvi would have to have taken if he really had ended his own life at the end of the orange rope.

"The detectives were not interested in the factors that had already convinced Carlo Calvi that his father could not possibly have killed himself this way. Roberto Calvi was 62 when he died, overweight, and a chronic sufferer from vertigo. In the pitch darkness he would have had to spot the scaffolding under the bridge, practically submerged in the high tide, stuff his pockets and trouser flies with bricks, clamber over a stone parapet and down a 12 ft-long vertical ladder, then edge his way eight feet along the scaffolding. He would then have had to gingerly lower himself to another scaffolding pole before putting his neck in the noose and throwing himself off, because both inquests noted that there was minimal damage to the neck, indicating he had not dropped a long way."

Kroll Associates was "not interested in what was probable," noted an account of the case by London's *The Independent*, "only in what was unavoidable." "They had their Calvi stand-in wear the same kind of loafers the banker was wearing when he died, then maneuver his way onto the scaffolding by the various possible routes: after which the shoes were soaked in water for the same length of time as Calvi's.

"Each time the test was tried, microscopic examination of the shoes by a forensic chemist picked up traces of the yellow paint with which the scaffolding poles were stained. Because the shoes Calvi was wearing when he died betrayed no such traces, Kroll concluded, 'Someone else had to have tied him to the scaffolding and killed him.'

"As a result of Carlo Calvi's long campaign to clear his father from the dishonor of suicide, in September 2003 City of London Police reopened the case as a murder inquiry. Detective Superintendent Trevor Smith asserted, 'We have been applying 21st century forensics and investigative techniques to a twenty-one-year-old crime.'"

The murder investigation would lead police, the general public, and Catholics into the modern manifestation of the two-thousand-year-old religion symbolized by the Vatican and, at the same time, unravel the mysterious life of the victim.

A cold, shy, stubborn man from the mountains north of Milan, Roberto Calvi in his prime was one of the most brilliant bankers in Italy. He had risen rapidly in the ranks of the private Banco Ambrosiano, which had been founded by a priest and had long had close relations with the Vatican's bank, Istituto per le Opere di Religione.

"For all his brilliance," wrote journalists Peter Popham and Philip Willan in Rome and Robert Verkaik for the *Annotico Report* in June 2007, "Calvi landed in desperate trouble. As well as co-operating closely with the Vatican's bankers, he also got into bed with the Sicilian Mafia, setting up a network of offshore shell companies which enabled them to launder the proceeds of the heroin trade."

Calvi was a "member of P2, the secret Masonic lodge to which hundreds of Italian politicians, businessmen, secret service agents, policemen, civil servants" and high officials of the Vatican belonged, that Pope John Paul I had been determined to drive from the Holy See.

The Roman Catholic Church and Freemasonry had long been at loggerheads. The first public written attack on Masons was made on April 28, 1738, by Pope Clement XII in his decree *In eminenti*. "The principal objections to Freemasonry were: that it was open to men of all religions; that oaths were taken; that Masons denied clerical authority, and that Masons met in secret. Clement banned Masonic membership by Catholics and directed 'Inquisitors of Heretical Depravity' to take action against Catholics who became Masons or assisted Freemasonry in any way. He ordered excommunication as punishment for those who defied his ban."

In an address by Pope Pius IX, *Multiplices inter*, on September 25, 1865, the pontiff renewed condemnation of Freemasonry and other secret societies. In it, he accused Masonic associations of conspiracy against the Church, God, and society. He attributed revolutions and uprisings to Masonic activities, and denounced Masonry's secret oaths and clandestine meetings.

On February 15, 1882, Leo XIII's encyclical *Etsi nos* referred to a "pernicious sect" at war with Jesus Christ. Two years later in *Humanum genus*

(April 20, 1884), the most vicious attack on Freemasonry of any papal pronouncements stated, "The Masonic sect produces fruits that are pernicious and of the bitterest savor." It went on to say that "Freemasonry's goal was the destruction of the Roman Catholic Church, and that Freemasonry and the Roman Catholic Church were adversaries." It further stated that "many Freemasons were unaware of the ultimate goals of Freemasonry and should not be considered partners in the criminal acts perpetrated by Freemasonry. He also condemned the naturalism of Freemasonry, by which is meant the belief that 'human nature and human reason ought in all things to be mistress and guide.' American Masonic leader Albert Pike stated that this encyclical was a "declaration of war, and the signal for a crusade, against the rights of man."

In the 1917 Code of Canon Law, the Church incorporated the attitude of many previous papal encyclicals into statutory law. In Canon 2335 of the 1917 Code, the Church held that "those who joined a Masonic sect, or other societies of the same sort, plot against the Church" incurred excommunication.

On November 26, 1983, the same year that the church adopted a new Canon of Church Law, the Congregation for the Doctrine of the Faith said that "the Church's negative position on Masonic associations" ... remained unaltered, since the principles had always been regarded as irreconcilable with the Church." It stated, "Catholics enrolled in masonic associations are involved in serious sin and may not approach holy communion."

By 1978, the Masonic group P2 "had become a sort of state within the Italian state, manipulating the direction of the country from a strong right-wing position, exerting a profound but long undetected influence on government decision making. The Vatican, the Mafia, P2; three drastically diverse worlds, linked by the fact that Italy was, throughout the Cold War a key frontline player in East–West relations, and possessor of the biggest Communist Party in Western Europe.

"According to one of the more persuasive theories swirling around the Calvi case," noted authors Peter Popham, Philip Willan, and Robert Verkaik, "the Milanese banker became a pivotal player not only in the laundering of Mafia money but in the secret channeling of large sums from the Vatican to the struggle of the Polish trade union Solidarity against Poland's Communist government."

"Since the accession to the papacy of the Polish cardinal Karol Wojtyła in 1978, [aiding Solidarity] had become a matter of vital importance for the Vatican." As the successor to St. Peter, who had been crucified upside down by the tyranny that was the Roman Empire, Pope John Paul II had begun a personal crusade to break the tyrannical stranglehold of the Soviet Union on his native Poland by showing that the Polish trade union Solidarity had the support of the Pope.

The Soviet dictator Joseph Stalin had once been asked if he was worried about what Pope Pius XII might have to say about aggression by the Red Army. Stalin had cynically replied, "How many divisions does the pope have?"

John Paul II planned to show Stalin's successor that Pope John Paul II did not need troops. His weapons were words—and money.

"Founded in 1942 to invest and increase the funds given to the Holy See for religious works, the [Istituto per le Opere di Religione] I.O.R., ... better known as the Vatican bank," was similar to any other international commercial bank. Located in the "medieval tower of Sixtus V, ... it accepted savings and checking accounts, transferred funds in and out of the Vatican, and made investments. Depositors had to be in some way connected with the Vatican. The list of those eligible included members of the Curia (the Pope had a personal account, No. 16/16), the 729 permanent residents of Vatican City, and a small group of clergymen and laymen doing regular business with the Vatican." As *Time* magazine noted, "No others need apply."

Laundering Vatican money through Latin America, mostly in Panama, in order to provide millions to the Solidarity movement, the Vatican also helped the Central Intelligence Agency to channel money to anticommunist groups, such as the Contras in Nicaragua. The Vatican's main conduit was Banco Ambrosiano, Italy's largest privately owned bank. Its chairman Roberto Calvi, shuffled money between his vaults and the IOR.

Known as God's banker, Calvi was "one of the men who knew a lot about a lot," noted authors Popham, Willan, and Verkaik. For years Calvi "handled the affairs of his highly disparate clients with flair, rewarding them with fat rates of interest, managing the illegal funding of political parties, playing the midwife to secret arms deals, and laundering Mafia profits." Key to the high-rolling success of such deals was his network of offshore shell companies.

"A man who later boasted that he taught Calvi all he knew about tax havens, the Sicilian financier Michele Sindona was reckless in a way that Calvi had never been. The two became ever more closely tied by secret financial favors—but when an American bank Sindona controlled, Franklin National Bank of New York, collapsed in 1974, Calvi refused to bail him out to the extent Sindona believed he deserved. He began putting pressure on Calvi to give more, pressure that soon yielded negative publicity about Calvi, prompting the Bank of Italy to send in inspectors.

"In 1978 the Bank of Italy had concluded that Calvi's Banco Ambrosiano had exported several billion lire illegally, prompting a criminal investigation. The Banco Ambrosiano was suddenly in meltdown, and Roberto Calvi's nightmare was under way. On May 20, 1981, finance police officers rang Calvi's doorbell at dawn with the news that the banker was under arrest and would be taken to prison. Inside, he attempted suicide.

"Convicted of currency law violation, Calvi was given a suspended four-year sentence. But his troubles were only beginning." The bank, it was revealed, "was hundreds of millions of dollars in debt. In terror of being imprisoned again, fearful also that mafiosi to whom he owed hundreds of millions would take their revenge, he went on the run. Escorted by...Flavio Carboni, a playboy and property developer, and Silvano Vittor, a smuggler based in Trieste who acted as his bodyguard, he left Italy under a false identity, traveling by speedboat to Yugoslavia, from there to Austria and by private plane to Britain. In London, he checked into a cheap residential hotel, the Chelsea Cloisters, and remained incommunicado."

Subsequent investigations indicated that Calvi was "lured to London, where he had been handed over to...members of Italian organized crime. Carboni, a Sardinian businessman with links to former Italian prime min-

ister Silvio Berlusconi; imprisoned Mafia boss Pippo Calo; former contra-
band smuggler Vittor; and Roman loan shark Ernesto Diotallevi conspired together to murder Calvi...to punish him for losing money that
belonged to the Cosa Nostra and to prevent him from blackmailing former accomplices in the Vatican, the P2 Masonic lodge and Italian political parties. According to a Mafia informant, Calo engaged an assassin
called Francesco di Carlo to carry out the murder....Mafia turncoat
Antonino Giuffre...accused Carboni of playing the traitor's role in a classic Mafia murder conspiracy: first gaining Calvi's confidence and then de-
livering him for execution....The Mafia accountant, Calo, accused of
ordering the killing to punish Calvi for embezzling Cosa Nostra's funds,"
said later that "he would never have turned to the men [responsible]...for
strangling Calvi if he knew they were in rival organizations or were
banned in disgrace from Cosa Nostra." At trial, the judge ordered the ac-
quittal of four defendants for lack of proof.

Before Mafia assassins tracked down Roberto Calvi, God's banker
placed the worth of the Vatican Bank to be in excess of $10 billion. In May
1981, the Italian police raided the home of P2 Grand Master Licio Gelli
and found a list of P2 Masons that included names of fifty-two members
of the Italian government. Investigators tracing transactions between
dummy corporations and Swiss bank accounts set up by Calvi followed
the flow of money to P2 and found that the Solidarity movement had got-
ten more than $100 million.

Assistance to the anti-communists in Poland by Pope John Paul II that
went far beyond words and moral support did not go unnoticed in the
Kremlin.

CHAPTER 7

From Russia with Malice

A Vatican biography of Pope John Paul II noted he was born in the Polish town of Wadowice on May 18, 1920, the youngest of three children born to Karol Wojtyła and Emilia Kaczorowska. He was baptized on June 20, 1920, in the parish church, "made his First Holy Communion at age 9, and was confirmed at 18. Upon graduation from Marcin Wadowita High School in Wadowice, he enrolled in Krakow's Jagiellonian University in 1938 and in a school for drama."

"The Nazi occupation forced closure of the university in 1939, and he had to work in a quarry (1940–44) and then in the Solvay chemical factory to earn his living and to avoid being deported to Germany.... Aware of his call to the priesthood, he began courses in the clandestine seminary of Krakow, run by Cardinal Adam Stefan Sapieha, archbishop of Krakow. At the same time, Karol Wojtyła was one of the pioneers of the clandestine 'Rhapsodic Theater.'"

"After the Second World War, he continued his studies in the major seminary of Krakow, once it had re-opened, and in the faculty of theology of the Jagiellonian University. He was ordained to the priesthood by Archbishop Sapieha in Krakow on November 1, 1946. Shortly afterward, Cardinal Sapieha sent him to Rome where he worked under the guidance of a French Dominican. He finished his doctorate in theology in 1948 with a thesis on the subject of faith in the works of St. John of the Cross ('Doctrina de fide apud Sanctum Ioannem a Cruce'). At that time, during his vacations, he exercised his pastoral ministry among the Polish immigrants of France, Belgium and Holland....

"In 1948 he returned to Poland and was vicar of various parishes in Krakow as well as chaplain to university students until 1951, when he took up again his studies in philosophy and theology. In 1953 he defended a thesis on 'evaluation of the possibility of founding a Catholic ethic on the ethical system of Max Scheler' at Lublin Catholic University. Later he became professor of moral theology and social ethics in the major seminary of Krakow and in the Faculty of Theology of Lublin.

"On July 4, 1958, he was appointed titular bishop of Ombi and auxiliary of Krakow by Pope Pius XII, and was consecrated September 28, 1958, in Wawel Cathedral, Krakow. On January 13, 1964, he was appointed archbishop of Krakow by Pope Paul VI, who made him a cardinal June 26, 1967" with the title of S. Cesareo in Palatio of the order of deacons, later elevated to the order of priests.

"Besides taking part in Vatican Council II [1962–65] where he made an important contribution to drafting the *Constitution Gaudium et spes*, Cardinal Wojtyła participated in all the assemblies of the Synod of Bishops." The Cardinals elected him Pope at the Conclave of October 16, 1978, and he took the name of John Paul II. On October 22, he solemnly inaugurated his Petrine ministry as the 263rd pope. "At the age of 58, he was the youngest pope of the twentieth century" and the first non-Italian pope since the fifteenth century. He brought to the Vatican a burning opposition to Communism and a fervor to liberate Poland.

"As John Paul II set foot on his native soil, at the Okecie military airport, he fell on his knees and kissed the ground. He was greeted by the hated Polish head of state, Henryk Jablonski, and the Polish Primate, Cardinal Stefan Wyszynski. The Pope was driven into Warsaw in an open-top car, he was welcomed by two-million people cheering 'Long live our Pope.' He was greeted by a further 250,000 people as he entered Victory Square for an open-air Mass. Many wept as he walked up to the altar and stood with open arms before a 30 ft cross draped in red."

In an exchange of speeches with Jablonski, the Polish Communist's knees were shaking. John Paul II said his visit was dictated by strictly religious motives, but he stressed that he hoped that his visit would help the "internal unity of my fellow countrymen and also a further favorable development of relations between the state and the church in my beloved motherland."

He told the throng, and a world watching via television, "I have kissed the ground of Poland on which I grew up, the land from which, through the inscrutable design of providence, God called me to the chair of Peter in Rome, the land from which I am coming today as a pilgrim."

Watching the spectacle on television in Moscow, grim-faced officials of the Soviet Union's espionage service, the KGB, heard the Pope say, "It is not possible to understand the history of the Polish nation without Christ."

The men in KGB headquarters recognized a threat.

It materialized in August 1980 when Polish workers demonstrated defiance of the Communist authorities by going on strike at the Lenin shipyard in the port city of Gdansk. "Festooned with flowers, white and red Polish flags and portraits of Pope John Paul II," said one international press account, "the plant's iron gates came to symbolize that heady mixture of hope, faith and patriotism that sustained the workers through their vigil."

"In September 1981," the leader of the shipbuilders' strike, Lech Walesa, "was elected Chairman of the First National Solidarity Congress in Gdansk. As the world watched and wondered if Soviet tanks would put an end to it all, Walesa and his fellow strikers stood their ground. Like soldiers before battle, they confessed to priests and received Communion in the open shipyard. To reduce the risk of violence, Walesa called for a ban on alcohol and insisted on strict discipline. . . .

"The government team finally gave in on almost all of the workers' demands. In addition to the right to strike and form unions, the Warsaw regime . . . reduced state censorship and access to broadcasting networks for the unions and the Church. At a nationally televised ceremony, where strikers and government representatives stood side by side and sang the Polish national anthem, Walesa signed what became known as the Gdansk agreement with a giant souvenir pen bearing the likeness of John Paul II."

In January 1981, the KGB noted Walesa being received by Pope John

Paul II in the Vatican. Falling to his knees, "Walesa kissed the papal ring and then briefly resisted the Pope's efforts to pull him to his feet. The union leader then had a rare private meeting with the Pope, which lasted for half an hour." When they emerged, the Pope said, " 'I wish to assure you that during your difficulties I have been with you in a special way, above all through prayer.' He declared that the right to form free associations was 'one of the fundamental human rights.' "

In Poland, "as workers rushed to join up at hastily improvised union locals across the country, Walesa and the other ex-strike leaders quickly found themselves at the head of a labor federation that soon grew to 10 million members—fully a quarter of the Polish population.... Walesa insisted that Solidarity should be a simple labor movement, not a political opposition. On the day he arrived at a Gdansk apartment building to open Solidarity's first makeshift headquarters, a wooden crucifix under his arm and a bouquet of flowers in his hand, he told a group of reporters, 'I am not interested in politics, I am a union man. My job now is to organize the union.' "... The KGB men who knew about revolutions thought otherwise.

"The country was soon swept by a spate of wildcat strikes over local issues. In some cases the Solidarity chapters were taking on the Communist Party bureaucracy by demanding the ouster of corrupt local officials or the conversion of party buildings to public hospitals.... As rank-and-file militants threatened to spin out of Walesa's control, [he pleaded,] 'We must concentrate on basic issues. There's a fire in the country.'

"All the while, the Kremlin watched with rising anxiety. Solidarity's existence was incompatible with the Communist Party's monopoly of power.... Even more important, the drive for democracy within the Polish party challenged the Leninist doctrine of centralized party discipline. Poland's festering economic crisis also put a strain on the entire Soviet bloc.... The 'Polish disease,' [as the men in the Kremlin called it,] might infect other ... countries ... [and threaten] the future of the Soviet empire."

In a report on John Paul II's visit to New York in 1979, *Time* magazine noted, "The Pontiff is emerging as the kind of incandescent leader that the world so hungers for—one who can make people feel that they have been lifted above the drabness of their own lives and show them that they are capable of better emotions, and better deeds, than they may have thought."

The physically vigorous pontiff was "a man for all seasons, all situations, all faiths, a beguilingly modest superstar of the church. The professional philosopher read [to] the diplomats of the United Nations a closely reasoned intellectual sermon on the importance of human rights and freedom—and offered in contrast the ghastly memory of Auschwitz in his homeland." The "athlete-outdoorsman" maintained a schedule "that would have stunned many a man of far fewer years than his 59, and he seemed impervious to the driving rains that fell on his motorcades in Boston and Manhattan." The man who had been an actor before entering the priesthood "displayed a sure command of smile, gesture and wink, and capitalized on a thick Polish accent to draw a laughing cheer by voicing admiration for Manhattan's 'sky-scroppers.'..."

"The humanitarian pastor delighted in the happiness of his flock, said the *Time* article, and he became one with them. Children were his special favorites, and he swept them up lightly in his brawny arms. When a young monsignor from Harlem bent to kiss his ring, John Paul lifted him to his feet and kissed him on both cheeks."

Said Billy Graham, "He's the most respected religious leader in the world today." President Carter welcomed John Paul II at a Saturday afternoon ceremony on the White House lawn with "God blessed America by sending you to us."

To cold-eyed men in KGB offices in Moscow, John Paul II was not a godsend who resided in a palace with walls, corridors and rooms ornately decorated with the masterpieces of the world's greatest artists, but a troublemaker holding an office in a Vatican that had strong, but secret, ties to the American intelligence services. The KGB men took notice that when Ronald Reagan took office as president, he chose as head of the CIA a Roman Catholic and member of the Sovereign Military Order of Malta (SMOM).

Founded in A.D. 1080 as Crusaders, the Knights of Malta "historically had been the military arm of the Vatican and was regarded as a separate state with full powers of statehood, including issuing its own diplomatic passports." It was said that in more recent decades SMOM acted as a funding conduit, a money laundry for the CIA, and the Vatican's intelligence agency. "Malta knighthoods were awarded to many leading individuals who were part of the military and intelligence community."

President Reagan's choice as CIA Director was William Casey. Other Knights of Malta in the Reagan administration were former NATO general and later secretary of state Alexander Haig and presidential advisor General Vernon Walters, a former deputy director of the CIA under George H. W. Bush, and later a roving ambassador.

The relationship between the U.S. intelligence community, the Vatican, and the SMOM began when the legendary head of the World War II Office of Strategic Services (OSS, the precursor of the CIA) was knighted by Pope Pius XII. William "Wild" Bill Donovan was made a Knight along with his wartime compatriot and later CIA Chief of Counterintelligence, James Jesus Angleton. "Donovan was ushered into an ornate chamber in Vatican City for an audience with Pope Pius XII" and decorated with the Grand Cross of the Order of Saint Sylvester. The oldest and most prestigious of papal knighthoods, this rarely bestowed "award was given to men who 'by feat of arms or writings or outstanding deeds have spread the Faith and have safeguarded and championed the Church.'"

Donovan was deemed worthy because of services he rendered to the Catholic hierarchy in World War II. "In 1941, the year before OSS was officially constituted, Donovan forged an alliance with Father Felix Morlion, the founder of a European Catholic intelligence service known as Pro Deo. When the Germans overran Western Europe, Donovan helped Morlion move his base of operations from Lisbon to New York. From then on, Pro Deo was financed by Donovan, who believed that it would result in insights into the secret affairs of the Vatican" and provide a window into the activities of the Fascist government of Benito Mussolini. "When the Allies liberated Rome in 1944, Morlion reestablished a spy network in the Vatican."

"For centuries, the Vatican was a prime target of foreign espionage. One of the world's greatest repositories of raw intelligence, it was a spy's gold mine. Ecclesiastical, political and economic information filtered in from thousands of priests, bishops and the papal nuncios of the Office of the Papal Secretariat. So rich was this source of intelligence that after the war, the CIA created a special unit in its counterintelligence section to tap it and monitor developments within the Vatican....

"Since World War II, the CIA was reported to have subsidized a Catholic lay organization that served as a political slugging arm of the pope and the Vatican throughout the Cold War; penetrated the American section of one of the wealthiest and most powerful Vatican orders (Knights of Malta); and passed money to a large number of priests and bishops— some of whom became witting [an agent who knows he reports to an agency of the U.S. government] agents in CIA covert operations. They employed undercover operatives to lobby members of the Curia and spy on liberal churchmen on the pope's staff who challenged the political as- sumptions of the United States; and prepared intelligence briefings that accurately predicted the rise of liberation theology." The CIA also collab- orated with Catholic groups to counter actions of leftist clerics in Latin America.

"In February 1981, just over a year following his triumphal visit to the United States, Pope John Paul II planned to refuel for three hours in Anchorage, Alaska, en route home following a major pastoral trip to the Philippines, Japan, and Guam. When the White House learned of this plan, National Security Council staffers recommended that Reagan 'establish an early, personal relationship with the Pope while welcoming him back to North American soil.' On February 5, NSC staffer James M. Rentschler proposed that a 'Nanook-of-the-North mission' be mounted during the pope's Alaskan layover.

"Accordingly, when John Paul landed in Anchorage on February 25, the envoy-designate to the Vatican, William Wilson, handed him a letter from Reagan, stating: '...I hope you will not hesitate to use [Wilson] as the channel for sensitive matters you or your associates may wish to com- municate to me.'"

Three moths later, John Paul II was being driven slowly around St. Peter's Square in his open jeep to greet thousands of people who crowded into Vatican City to see him and receive his blessing. On May 13, 1981, dressed in a papal-white cassock, he was shaking hands and lifting small children into his arms. As he reached a point just outside the Vatican's bronze gate, there was a burst of gunfire.

"One hand rising to his face and blood staining his garments," reported the *New York Times*, "the Pope faltered and fell into the arms of his Polish secretary, the Rev. Stanislaw Dziwisz, and his personal servant, Angelo Gugel, who were in the vehicle with him....

Rushed by an ambulance to Gemelli Hospital, two miles north of the Vatican, for surgery,...John Paul was conscious as he was taken to the operating room....

"The gunman had fired four times in the attack. Two tourists, an American and a Jamaican, were wounded by two of the bullets. The gunman, armed with a nine-millimeter Browning automatic, was set upon by bystanders, who knocked the pistol out of his hand. He was arrested, taken away by police car, and later identified as twenty-three-year-old Mehmet Ali Agca. Police quoted him as having told them, 'My life is not important.'

"He was said to have arrived in Italy the previous Saturday at the Milan airport and arrived in Rome on Monday. The police said that he had in his pocket several notes in handwritten Turkish, one of them saying, 'I am killing the Pope as a protest against the imperialism of the Soviet Union and the United States and against the genocide that is being carried out in El Salvador and Afghanistan.'

"The Turkish news agency Anatolia reported that Agca had been convicted of murdering Abdi Ipekci, the editor of the Turkish newspaper *Milliyet*, in February 1979, but had escaped from prison later that year. Anatolia said he wrote a letter to the newspaper on Nov. 26, 1979, saying that he had fled from prison with the intention of killing the Pope, who was due to visit Ankara and Istanbul....

"The Vatican announced that the Pope...had suffered multiple lesions of the abdomen and a massive hemorrhage and had been given a transfusion of about six pints of blood. The Vatican also said that he had been wounded in the right forearm and the second finger of his left hand."

Some news media quickly assumed the plot was the work of Turkish terrorists known as the Gray Wolves, a neo-Nazi group of both former military and Islamist extremists. This theory surfaced within hours of the arrest of Agca. Later, authorities investigating the attack declared it had been directed by the Bulgarian secret service, "acting on orders from the Soviet Union. This accusation depended on the secret confession of [Agca]....As he was taken from a Rome police station, Agca surprised waiting reporters by publicly implicating the Soviets in the conspiracy. He said, 'The KGB organized everything.'

"In a chaotic encounter outside the police station, the slim, unshaven Turk, speaking in broken English and flawed Italian, claimed that he was trained as a terrorist 'in Bulgaria and in Syria.' Italian officials believed that he was aided in the assassination attempt by three Bulgarians: two former employees at [Bulgaria's] Rome embassy and Sergei Ivanov Antonov, onetime Rome manager of the Bulgarian airline. 'Was Antonov involved?' newsmen asked, as Agca climbed into a police van. 'I knew Sergei,' Agca replied. 'He was my accomplice.'

'And the KGB?' 'Yes, the KGB.'"

In 2008, "Claire Sterling, a prize-winning journalist and author, had just published *The Terror Network* when Ali Agca tried to kill the pope.... Miss Sterling had quickly seen the Bulgarian connection when it became known that Agca had made several trips to Sofia, Bulgaria, and stayed in a hotel favored by the Bulgarian KGB. In Rome he had also had contacts with a Bulgarian agent whose cover was the Bulgarian national airline office.

"*The Time of the Assassin*, published in 1983, was Miss Sterling's in-depth look at the plot to kill Pope John Paul II and the subsequent investigation. She had no doubt the plot originated at 2 Dzerzhinsky Square, KGB headquarters in Moscow. The KGB assigned this super-wet operation to the Bulgarians....The Bulgarians then looked for cover and deniability among a Turkish extremist group involved with the KGB in lucrative drug smuggling routes through Bulgaria to Western Europe."

President Reagan and CIA Director William Casey decided to play down the Soviet link. Reagan had survived an assassination attempt on March 30, 1981, as he left the Washington Hilton Hotel. He and Casey feared any administration hint of Soviet involvement in the plot to kill the pope might upset U.S.-Soviet relations, and conspiracy theorists would quickly conclude the KGB had also targeted Reagan.

Shortly after John Paul was released from the hospital, he visited Agca in prison. Sentenced to serve nineteen years, Agca was released early and sent back to Turkey to stand trial on an earlier unrelated charge. The pontiff later told old friends on two occasions that he was also satisfied the hand behind the plot was in Moscow.

During his trial, "Ali Agca feigned madness by declaring he had acted on God's instructions. He later claimed to be the new messiah and to have conspired with Vatican prelates who recognized him as deity. Italian psychiatrists concluded he had been instructed to play the fool as a way of hiding Bulgaria's—Moscow's—tracks.

The Italian examining-magistrate in charge of the investigation, Ferdinando Imposimato, told Italian radio, 'I believe Agca said many true things, but then he tried to torpedo the trial after being threatened inside prison by a Bulgarian agent who got inside to make sure he would retract his allegations.'"

Later, "*Corriere della Sera*, Italy's most influential daily newspaper, disclosed new documents found in the files of former East German intelligence services which confirmed the 1981 assassination plot was ordered by the Soviet KGB and then assigned to the Bulgarian satellite service. Metodi Andreev, a former official in charge of the Bulgarian KGB's files [reportedly] said he had seen correspondence between Stasi, the East German service, and the Bulgarian agents. These included an order from the KGB to pull out all the stops to bury Bulgaria's connection to the plot." Bulgaria then handed the execution of the plot to Turkish extremists, including Mehmet Ali Agca, who pulled the trigger. On the Pope's sixty-first birthday (May 22, 1981), Reagan sent Congressman Peter Rodino to Rome with a personal letter for John Paul, who was still hospitalized after the attempt on his life. Having also been shot in the chest in an assassination attempt on March 30, Reagan wrote, "The qualities you exemplify remain a precious asset as we confront the growing dangers of the moment."

"On December 12–13, 1981, the Communist government of Poland arrested thousands of Solidarity activists. Over the next weeks the White House and the Vatican consulted closely on the events in Poland by telephone, cable, and through diplomatic representatives...

"The United States will not let the Soviet Union dictate Poland's future with impunity," Reagan wrote the Pope on December 29, 1981. "I am announcing today additional American measures aimed at raising the cost to the Russians of their continued violence against Poland."

"A week later," Ambassador Wilson was handed a letter from John Paul II to Reagan "pledging support for the U.S. sanctions. Though John Paul worried about the impact of sanctions on the Polish people, he said that he would stand with Reagan, even if he could not say so publicly."

A cable to Haig said, "The Vatican recognizes that the U.S. is a great power with global responsibilities. The United States must operate on the political plane and the Holy See does not comment on the political positions taken by governments. It is for each government to decide its political policies. The Holy See for its part operates on the moral plane, [but] both the Holy See and the United States have the same objective: the restoration of liberty to Poland."

On June 7, 1982, President Reagan arrived at the Vatican to meet with John Paul. Reporter and author Carl Bernstein wrote, "It was the first time the two had met, and they talked for fifty minutes. In the same wing of the papal apartments, Agostino Cardinal Casaroli and Archbishop Achille Silvestrini met with Secretary of State Alexander Haig and Judge William Clark, Reagan's National Security Adviser."

In that meeting in the Pope's private library, Reagan and John Paul II agreed to undertake a secret campaign for the dissolution of the Communist empire.

Said Richard Allen, Reagan's first National Security Adviser, "This was one of the great secret alliances of all time."

According to aides who shared their leaders' view of the world, Bernstein noted, Reagan and John Paul II "refused to accept a fundamental political fact of their lifetimes—the division of Europe as mandated at the Yalta [a conference in 1945] and the Communist dominance of Eastern Europe. A free Poland...would be a dagger to the heart of the Soviet empire." If Poland became democratic, other East European states would follow. This secret Vatican meeting cemented the foundation for an outright war with Soviet Communism, with the USA and the Holy See as allies.

On January 10, 1984, the Reagan administration established full diplomatic relations with the Vatican, ending more than a century of official separation, but often secret contacts, between the White House and Vatican.

History has recorded that the friendship between the Pope and the president that Richard Allen called "one of the great secret alliances of all time," sealed with a handshake in the Vatican, resulted in the liberation of Poland, the fall of the Iron Curtain, the dissolution of the Soviet Union, the demise of Communism in Europe, and the end of the Cold War.

CHAPTER 8

Opus Dei: The Pope's Cult

The vast majority of Americans, and many, if not most, Roman Catholics in the United States never heard of Opus Dei before the publication of Dan Brown's novel *The Da Vinci Code* or until the film version opened in theaters from coast to coast. The sensational book and movie introduced Opus Dei in the form of an albino priest committing a murder in the Louvre Museum in Paris.

At the zenith of *The Da Vinci Code* phenomenon, *Time* magazine noted that the book depicted Opus Dei as "a powerful and ultraconservative Roman Catholic faction riddled with sadomasochistic ritual....In its 78 years, Opus Dei was a rumor magnet. Successful and secretive, it was accused of using lavish riches" and influence in the Vatican "to do everything from propping up Francisco Franco's Spanish dictatorship to pushing through" rapid beatification for its founder in 1992, only seventeen years after his death.

Declared by Pope John Paul II to be a "personal prelature" in 1982, Opus Dei, meaning "God's work," has been called a "global quasi-diocese, able in some cases to leapfrog local archbishops and deal directly with [the Pope in] Rome.

Opus Dei states that it is a Catholic institution with a mission to spread "the message that work and the circumstances of everyday life are occasions for growing closer to God, for serving others, and for improving society."

Critics say it's a dangerous, if not malevolent, religious cult.

Wherein lies the truth?

On October 2, 1928, in Spain, twenty-six-year-old Josemaría Escrivá envisioned "a movement of pious laypeople who would, by prayerful contemplation and steady dedication of their labor to Christ, extend the holiness of going to church on Sunday into their everyday work life.... He saw Opus eventually acting as 'an intravenous injection [of holiness] in the bloodstream of society.' "

In the wake of the publication of *The Da Vinci Code*, and the description of Opus Dei in the novel as a sinister and malevolent group, *Time* reported, "Opus Dei is not a kind of spiritual pick-me-up for casual Catholics. It features a small, committed membership (85,500 worldwide and a mere 3,000 in the U.S.), many of whom come from pious families and are prepared to embrace unpopular church teachings such as its birth-control ban. Members take part in a rigorous course of spiritual 'formation' stressing church doctrine and contemplation plus Escrivá's philosophy of work and personal holiness." Opus Dei says that it helps everyday people to "seek holiness in their work and ordinary activities."

According to the Opus Dei website, any lay Catholic may ask to join Opus Dei as long as he or she is at least eighteen years old. It takes about five years to join, with a person's commitment to joining having to be renewed each year, before a lifelong commitment is possible. Opus Dei has been described as "a strong advocate of traditional Catholic values, focusing on the spreading of the Catholic teaching that every individual is called to become a saint and an apostle of Jesus Christ and that ordinary life is a path to sanctity...."

"There are three types of members of Opus Dei: numeraries, associates and supernumeraries. Associates and numeraries make up about 25 percent to 30 percent of [the] members. They are celibate, live with other members and, on occasion, practice corporal mortification." This is the practice of physically enduring a minor amount of suffering. "Some of the celibate members of Opus Dei practice traditional Catholic penances such as using the cilice (a light metal chain with prongs which is worn round the thigh) and the discipline (a woven cotton strap). The motivation for these voluntary penances is to imitate Christ and to join in His redemptive sacrifice, and to suffer in solidarity with poor and deprived people all over the world." The majority of Opus Dei members are supernumeraries. They account for around three quarters of the members. They are usually noncelibate, married men or women.

In 1982, Pope John Paul II made Opus Dei the only "personal prelature" in the Catholic Church. This meant that Opus Dei's members were responsible only to Rome and God, not to local bishops. Opus Dei says "that this unique position does not in any way mean that its members are in specifically high regard by the Vatican, or given any special treatment. Personal prelature is a canonical term meaning that the jurisdiction of the Catholic Church over Opus Dei covers the members of Opus Dei, rather than a geographical area like a diocese. A personal prelature operates in a similar way to a religious order, however there are no geographical limits, and members are laypeople rather than monks or nuns.

"Those Catholics who belong to Opus Dei also continue to be part of the congregation at their local church. Unlike members of religious orders, the members of Opus Dei join by means of private contracts and not vows. In order to join members must ask to do so, and they must also be convinced that they have received a vocation. . . . Members have to donate a significant part of their income to Opus Dei. It is a decentralized organization and does not publish its general accounts." Critics have also described it as a sort of Catholic Freemasonry, accusing it of being secretive and manipulative. It has a special set of greetings: "Pax" and "In aeternum" ("Peace" and "In eternity"). Its 1950 constitution barred members from revealing their membership without getting permission from the director of their center. In 1982, a new document repudiated "secrecy or clandestine activity." Yet Opus did not identify its members, and many preferred not to identify themselves.

The American branch of Opus Dei noted that it began its apostolic activities "in Chicago in 1949, when Sal Ferigle, a young physics graduate student, and Fr. Joseph Muzquiz, one of the first three priests to be ordained for Opus Dei, arrived in Chicago. The first center was established near the University of Chicago. Today there are more than 3,000 members in the United States, and a great many more who participate in Opus Dei's activities of spiritual formation. These activities are organized from 60 centers in 19 cities: Boston; Chicago; Dallas; Delray Beach, Florida; Miami;

Milwaukee; New York; Pittsburgh; Princeton, New Jersey; Providence; St. Louis; San Antonio; Houston; Los Angeles; San Francisco; South Bend, Indiana; South Orange, New Jersey; Urbana, Illinois; and Washington, DC."

The Prelature of Opus Dei uses seven conference centers for retreats and seminars. They are located near Boston, Chicago, Houston, Miami, New York, San Francisco and Washington, DC.

Opus Dei members, in cooperation with others, operate one college and five secondary schools in the United States. They are Lexington College in Chicago, The Heights and Oakcrest near Washington, DC; Northridge Prep and The Willows near Chicago; and the Montrose School near Boston. Opus Dei also has residences for university students, the largest of which is Bayridge Residence for women in Boston. Other residences for university women are Petawa Residence in Milwaukee and Westfield Residence in Los Angeles. Residences for university men include Elmbrook Student Center in Boston; Lincoln Green in Champaign-Urbana, Illinois; Windmoor in South Bend; and Wingren in Dallas.

In 1991, Cardinal Joseph Bernardin, Archbishop of Chicago, entrusted the parish of St. Mary of the Angels to priests of Opus Dei. The Catholic Information Center in Washington, DC, and the Holy Cross Chapel in Houston, Texas, have also been entrusted to priests of Opus Dei.

Opus Dei's inconspicuous U.S. headquarters is a sedate red-brick $69 million, seventeen-story building at Lexington Avenue and Thirty-fourth street in Manhattan.

On October 6, 2002, Pope John Paul II elevated Escrivá to sainthood in a ceremony "watched by at least 300,000 of the priest's followers, who filled St Peter's Square and spilled into the surrounding streets and along the bank of the Tiber River. . . .

"The crowd was so quiet for most of the two-hour ceremony that they might have been holding their breath. It was surely one of the most decorous crowds ever to pack St. Peter's Square. They arrived in suits and ties, Burberry capes, and the occasional dinner jacket." The Pope, "dressed in white vestments, arrived at the square in his popemobile," built with bulletproof glass after the 1981 assassination attempt. Behind his stage, a giant image of the Catholic Church's newest saint was draped from the balcony of St. Peter's basilica. A relic of the saint, a fragment of his tooth, was placed next to the altar. At the climax of the ceremony, the 82-year-old pontiff said, 'With the authority of our Lord Jesus Christ, the saint apostles of Peter and Paul and our own, after a long reflection, many invocations of divine assistance, and having listened to the advice of many of our brother bishops, we declare and define blessed Josemaría Escrivá de Balaguer saint, and we will write his name in the album of the saints.'

"Many of the pilgrims attending the ceremony were from...Spain, but others came from Latin America, where Opus Dei had strongly taken hold. Spanish doctor Manuel Nevado Rey, whose recovery from radiation-caused skin disease was deemed a miracle performed by Escrivá, was among the crowd....Medical experts consulted by the Vatican said there was no scientific explanation for the transformation.

"The progression of Escrivá to sainthood was rapid. He was beatified, or made blessed, in 1992." He became the 468th saint to have been created by the Pope during his 24 years in office, more than those created by his predecessors over the past four centuries put together. "It was one of the fastest canonizations on record,...and one of the most controversial." "Escriva's path to sainthood was marred by charges that the Vatican refused to hear testimony from his critics."

Speculating that canonization of Escrivá transgressed canon law, *Newsweek* magazine religion correspondent Kenneth Woodward said that the Vatican's 'Devil's advocate' system," designed to slow down the canonization process by questioning the validity of the "miracle," "was bypassed when witnesses hostile to Opus Dei were not called." Opus Dei claimed that "eleven critics of Escrivá's canonization had been heard." Woodward said there was only one, and the "'consultors' were mainly Italian and members of Opus Dei: this stopped Escrivá's many critical Spanish peers from upsetting the canonization procedure."

What is more, said Opus Dei critics, it was "out of order for forty percent of the testimony to come from Escrivá's two henchmen, both of whom have since become Opus leaders....Dei allegedly pressured 'hundreds' of bishops, 'especially from the cash hungry third world,' to send favorable reports to Rome's saint makers. It was alleged that 1,300 Bishops sent in glowing reports, yet of these only 128 had personally met Escrivá."

Critics of Opus Dei in the United States pointed to "disgraced FBI agent, Robert Hanssen, who was jailed for life in 2001 for spying for the Russians over a fifteen-year period in return for payment of almost a million pounds, and was exposed as a devout Opus Dei member.... Hanssen's brother-in-law was reported to be an Opus Dei priest in Rome whose office was steps away from the pope."

Robert Hanssen's motive for his treachery was said to be a desire to afford the Opus Dei lifestyle and send his children to Opus schools. He allegedly justified his actions by the maxim of the Jesuit moral theology of the greater or lesser good.

In an article for *America, the National Catholic Monthly*, James Martin, S. J. noted that Opus Dei "is an increasingly strong presence on U.S. college campuses. Traditionally their efforts to attract new members had led them to colleges and universities. And it has sometimes led them into conflict with other campus Catholic groups." Donald R. McCrabb, executive director of the Catholic Campus Ministry Association, told McCrabb, "We are aware that Opus Dei is present at a number of campuses across the country. I'm also aware that some campus ministers find their activities on campus to be counterproductive."

One of the concerns was Opus Dei's emphasis on recruiting, supported by an apparently large base of funding. "They are not taking on the broader responsibility that a campus minister has." He also related, "I have heard through campus ministers that there's a spiritual director that's assigned to the candidate who basically has to approve every action taken by that person, including reading mail, what classes they take or don't take, what they read or don't read."

A former Columbia University student noted, "They recommended I not read some books, particularly the Marxist stuff, and instead use their boiled-down versions. I thought this was odd—I was required to do it for class!"

Susan Mountin, associate director of Marquette University's campus ministry, asserted that it was her sense "that there probably is a need for many people to experience some sort of devotion in their lives." What worried her was a "cult-like behavior, isolation from friends."

The director of campus ministry at Stanford University from 1984 through 1992, Russell J. Roide, S. J., told McCrabb that he initially approached Opus Dei with an open mind. However, students began coming to him complaining about Opus Dei's recruiting. "They just didn't let the students alone," he said. "Students would come to me and say, 'Please get them off our backs.'"

When he felt his only recourse was to pass out information to students about Opus Dei, including critical articles, Opus Dei numeraries visited Father Roide and said that he was "interfering with their agenda." Eventually, because of continued student complaints about recruiting, Roide decided "not to let them anywhere near the campus."

In 2003, an Internet posting claimed, "As part of its normal modus operandi, Opus Dei attempts to infiltrate and take over other mainstream Catholic organizations with the aim of turning them into recruitment fronts. Opus Dei will attempt to infiltrate both the leadership councils and the general memberships of any Catholic organization that it does not control. Such organizations can include, but are not limited to, young adult groups, CYO groups, college/university Newman Clubs, Campus Ministries, parishes, and schools. The purpose of this Guide is to provide tried and tested methods for maintaining the independence of Catholic groups and to prevent [an] Opus Dei takeover and destruction of other organs of the Catholic Church."

In April 2003, Elizabeth W. Green wrote in the *Harvard Crimson* that Harvard had produced "a steady stream of leaders in Opus Dei for nearly half a century, and over the past 40 years, at least three of those holding the highest position of authority within Opus Dei's U.S. branch were Harvard graduates." She asserted, "While Harvard students and graduates associated with the group say joining Opus Dei was the best thing they've ever done with their lives, others call it a dangerous trap, cult-like in its methods" that were "threatening in its caustic interpretation of Catholicism."

At the University of Notre Dame in South Bend, Indiana, reporter

Janice Flynn in *The Observer* online said in October 2004, "Students have taken an array of paths through Opus Dei. Some have deepened their spiritual lives. Others have had emotionally distressing experiences. All have been profoundly affected by the influence of Opus Dei while at Notre Dame."

Writing in the October/November 2004 *Washington Monthly*, Paul Baumann observed, "Many Catholics in Europe and in the United States regard the movement as politically reactionary, extreme in its spiritual and worldly ambition, and devious. The group's manner of 'recruiting,' especially of college students, has been criticized as overbearing or worse. There is even an organization, the Opus Dei Awareness Network, dedicated to exposing the group's methods. But Opus Dei has its admirers, who see it as a defender of traditional moral values, especially of the family, as well as a providential source of evangelical enthusiasm, orthodoxy, and unquestioned loyalty to Rome. Chief among those admirers was John Paul II, who presided over the speedy canonization of the movement's founder. Critics, however, saw Escrivá's 2002 canonization as a sure sign of the organization's ill-gotten wealth and malign influence."

After the death of John Paul II, as 115 cardinals met in conclave to name a successor, Opus Dei members knew there was no guarantee he would treat Opus Dei with the favor Pope John Paul II had bestowed upon it. "Their basic concern is that they might actually end up among the big losers," said John Allen, correspondent for the *National Catholic Reporter*. But the men and women within Opus Dei insisted its future was secure. A spokesman dismissed the possibility a new pope would turn against it. Opus Dei's vision of involving laypeople further in the Church, he said, "is part of the DNA of the Church," and part of the reason for John Paul's backing. At stake was the influence of an organization that Allen estimated had assets worth $2.8 billion worldwide and $344.4 million in the United States.

New York Newsday staff correspondent Matthew McAllister noted, "If Opus Dei appears murky and alien to the world, that's partly because some of its practices can come across as throwbacks to the Middle Ages."

Noting that Opus Dei had flourished under John Paul II, David Yallop, author of *In God's Name: An Investigation into the Murder of Pope John Paul I,* wrote that if Benedict XVI is not a member of Opus Dei, he is everything Opus Dei adherents could wish a Pope to be. One of Benedict XVI's first acts as pontiff was to go to the tomb of Escrivá, pray, and bless a statue of him. He subsequently granted Opus Dei the status of personal prelature in Benedict's reign, retaining Opus Dei's status in which, Yallop noted, one becomes answerable only to the Pope and God.

Critics of Opus Dei also allege that it has connections with right-wing and pro-Nazi movements in Europe. Nothing in the recent history of the papacy has been more controversial than public and secret deals before and after World War II between Adolf Hitler's Nazi Germany and the Vatican.

CHAPTER 9

The Papacy and the Nazis

O n September 21, 2006, The *Catholic News Agency* (CNA) in Rome reported that "documents emerging from the Vatican's archives demonstrated that Cardinal Eugenio Pacelli, the future Pope Pius XII, defended anti-Nazi clergy and censured priests who expressed admiration for Adolf Hitler.

The CNA said, "German church historian Hubert Wolf told the Associated Press that the recorded minutes of Vatican meetings held in the late 1930s show that the ailing Pope Pius XI greatly relied on Cardinal Pacelli, then Secretary of State, to enforce his Pontificate's stance against Nazism and Fascism."

According to Wolf, the Pope (Pius XI) would "just make a blessing and say 'our secretary of state will find a solution.' "

"The archives, which spanned from 1922 to 1939, may offer answers into a controversy surrounding the cardinal who later became Pope, and who had been accused by some historians of failing to do enough to protect Jews during the Holocaust. The Vatican has insisted that Pius XII used discreet diplomacy that saved thousands of Jews." Much is known about the relationship between Pope Pius XII and the Nazis, but many believed that the Vatican archives contain documents and other evidence that would prove to be an embarrassment to the Church.

In the Vatican's official annals Pius XII, "who died in 1958, is painted as a saintly shepherd who led his flock with great moral courage in difficult times. For many scholars he was at worst the Devil incarnate, 'Hitler's Pope,' and at best a coward who refused to speak out against the extermination of Jews, gypsies and homosexuals in gas chambers, even when he had compelling evidence that it was happening, lest his words attract Nazi aggression."

In 2006, the British publication *The Independent* stated, "Month by month, year by year, more evidence emerges from other sources about where the Vatican's sympathies lay in the Second World War." What was known was "that in 1933, as the Vatican representative in Germany, the future Pius XII had agreed to a treaty with Hitler, whose authoritarian tendencies he admired, to close down the Catholic-dominated Center Party, one of National Socialism's staunchest opponents. This treaty was based on the Vatican's 1929 agreement with Mussolini, the Italian fascist leader. On being elected Pope in 1939, Pius XII suppressed a document denouncing Hitler that was titled *Mit brennender sorge* (*With Deep Anxiety*) that Pius XI had been writing on his deathbed. Throughout the war, Pius XII made no public condemnation of the Holocaust, except for a single ambiguous sentence in a 26-page Christmas message of 1942.

"Among various disputed accusations made against him were that he had done nothing to protect the Jews of Rome as the Nazis and Italian fascists carted them away to gas chambers.... that he forbade monasteries and convents to shelter Jews trying to escape the Nazis; that he allowed the Church to profit from looted goods taken from the Nazis' victims; and that he turned a blind eye to the assistance given by Catholic religious orders, notably in Croatia, to help Nazi war criminals escape to start new lives in Latin America," using what was called "the Rat line."

The Church vigorously denied all these charges, but historians argued that without access to the Vatican's wartime archives there could be no independent verification of the Vatican's claim that Pius XII was free from the stain of sin.

In 1999, British author John Cornwell's book, *Hitler's Pope*, "alleged that Pius [XII] was seemingly prepared to put up with any Nazi atrocity because he saw Hitler as a good bulwark against the advance across Europe of godless communism from Russia." He wrote that the future Pope "displayed anti-Semitic tendencies early on, and that his drive to promote papal absolutism inexorably led him to collaboration with fascist leaders. Cornwall convincingly depicted Cardinal Secretary of State Pacelli pursuing Vatican diplomatic goals that crippled Germany's large Catholic political party, which might otherwise have stymied Hitler's excesses.... Pacelli's failure to respond forcefully to the Nazis was more than a personal failure, said Cornwell, it was a failure of the papal office itself."

Apparently to counter Cornwell's book, the "Church agreed to allow access to a joint panel of six Jewish and Catholic experts, appointed by the Vatican and the International Jewish Committee for Inter-religious Consultation. By July 2001, the Jewish members of the group had resigned, quoting the 'lack of a positive response' from the Vatican."

In 2003, the Vatican announced it would permit "limited examination" of the documents related to Pius XII in the reading rooms of the Secret Vatican Archives and the Congregation for the Doctrine of the Faith. "Jewish leaders and scholars expressed considerable disappointment.... Pope John Paul II [was determined] to beatify Pius, who according to the Vatican did all he could to save lives, but did not take more public actions for fear of further endangering the Jews and Catholics in the Nazi-occupied countries.... The Vatican...maintained it would open the archives once they were put in order, it said the Pope had decided to open the archives 'to put an end to unjust and ungrateful speculation.'...

"John Paul II was the only one with the authority to open the archives and to release selected documents on ties between the Vatican and the Germans from 1922 to 1939, when the man who later became Pius XII was the Vatican's ambassador to Germany. Among the first of the wartime documents to be released, according [to the Vatican,] would be those dealing with Pius XII's 'charity and assistance' for those who were prisoners of war. 'We want historians to know the great activities of charity and assistance by Pius XII toward many prisoners and other war victims, including those of any nation, religion and race,' the statement read."

On August 13, 2003, reporter Laurie Goldstein of the *New York Times* reported that "diplomatic documents recently brought to light by a Jesuit historian indicated that while serving as a diplomat, the future pope expressed strong antipathy to the Nazi regime in private communication with American officials. One document was a confidential memorandum written in April 1938 from Cardinal Pacelli, who said...that compromise with the Nazis should be out of question." The other is a report by an American consul general relating that in a long conversation in 1937, Cardinal Pacelli called Hitler 'a fundamentally wicked person' and 'an untrustworthy scoundrel.'

"Historians who saw the documents said they bolstered the view that the man who became Pope Pius XII was not a Nazi sympathizer, and was in fact convinced that the Nazis were a threat to the church and the stability of Europe. But the historians agreed that the documents in no way explained or exonerated Pius XII's inaction in the face of the Holocaust." Neither document "mentioned the persecution of Jews that was well under way when they were written. The documents were described by Charles R. Gallagher, a Jesuit historian at St. Louis University, in an article in the Sept. 1 issue of *America*, the Jesuit weekly. Gallagher, 38, was a former police officer who was a nonordained Jesuit studying to be a priest. He said he came across them [the documents] while researching a biography about another more obscure papal diplomat....

"Mr. Gallagher said in an interview that he hoped the documents would illustrate that as a diplomat, Cardinal Pacelli made his case against the Nazis in private, to other diplomats. 'I wouldn't go so far as to say that these documents exonerate him,' he said. 'What I think these findings might help to dispel is the impression that this pope was, as others have called him, 'Hitler's Pope.'

"Mr. Gallagher found the Pacelli memorandum among the diplomatic papers of Ambassador Joseph P. Kennedy that were housed at the John F. Kennedy Presidential Library in Boston. Joseph Kennedy...served as ambassador to England from 1938 to 1940. Ambassador Kennedy received the memorandum in April 1938 when he met in Rome with Cardinal Pacelli, who was then the Vatican's secretary of state....The Cardinal also wrote that the church at times felt powerless and isolated in its daily struggle against all sorts of political excesses from the Bolsheviks to the new pagans arising among the young Aryan generations. He wrote that 'evidence of good faith' by the Nazi regime was 'completely lacking' and that 'the possibility of an agreement' with the Nazis was 'out of question for the time being.'"

Although the Vatican archives section dealing with the years of Pius XII's papacy had not yet been opened to historians in 2008, "in a speech to representatives from the US-based Pave the Way Foundation during their visit to his summer residence, Castel Gandolfo, [Pope Benedict XVI] said... that Pius XII 'spared no effort, wherever it was possible, to intervene (for Jews either) directly or through instructions given to individuals or institutions in the Catholic Church.'"

Benedict said Pius XII, "had to work 'secretly and silently' to 'avert the worst and save the highest number of Jews possible,'...repeating assertions made by Vatican experts in the past. The Pope also said Pius XII was thanked by Jewish groups during and after the war for saving the lives of thousands of Jews. He cited a meeting the leader of the Roman Catholic Church had in the Vatican in November 1945 at which 80 death camp survivors 'thanked him personally for his generosity.'" Benedict also said "further investigation would reinforce 'the historical truth, overcoming all remaining prejudice.'"

Benedict's defense came as the process begun by Pope John Paul II of canonizing Pius XII continued, and a few days before the fiftieth anniversary of Pius XII's death in 1958. Born in Rome in 1876, Eugenio Pacelli became a priest and obtained his first assignment as a "curate at Chiesa Nuova, the church where he had served as an altar boy. While there, he taught catechism to children....At the same time he pursued his studies for a doctorate in Canon Law and Civil Law...and he added doctorates in Philosophy and in Theology." In 1904, he "became a Papal Chamberlain with the title of Monsignor and one year later a Domestic Prelate....

"In 1908, Pacelli attended the Eucharistic Congress in London. The 32-year-old priest was by that time well embarked on what would become a nearly 40-year career of brilliant diplomatic service for the Church. From 1904 to 1916, he was a research aide in the Office of the Congregation of Extraordinary Ecclesiastical Affairs where he assisted Cardinal Pietro

Gasparri in the crucial task of clarifying and updating canon law. In 1910, Monsignor Pacelli was again back in London where he represented the Holy See at the Coronation of King George V.

"In 1911, Pope Pius X appointed Pacelli Undersecretary for Extraordinary Ecclesiastical Affairs. This department of the Secretariat of State, negotiated terms of agreements with foreign governments that would allow the Church to carry out its teaching mission. In 1912, he was appointed Secretary. Two years later, he became Secretary of the Congregation of Extraordinary Ecclesiastical Affairs."

When Pius X died in 1914, Pope Benedict XV appointed Monsignor Pacelli as Papal Nuncio to Bavaria, Germany. Before assuming the post, "he was consecrated a Bishop by Pope Benedict XV in the Sistine Chapel (May 13, 1917). He was then elevated to the rank of Archbishop and went to Germany to present his credentials to Ludwig III, King of Bavaria on May 28, 1917. American newspaper correspondent Dorothy Thompson, wrote: 'Those of us who were foreign correspondents in Berlin during the days of the Weimar Republic were not unfamiliar with the figure of the dean of the diplomatic corps. Tall, slender, with magnificent eyes, strong features and expressive hands, in his appearance and bearing Archbishop Pacelli looked every inch what he was, a Roman nobleman, of the proudest blood of the Western world. In knowledge of German and European affairs and in diplomatic astuteness, the Nuncio was without an equal.'…

"On June 22, 1920, Pacelli became the first Apostolic Nuncio to Germany. Four years later, March 29, 1924, he signed a concordat with Bavaria which was ratified by its Parliament on January 15, 1925. It determined the rights and duties of the Church and the government in respect to each other. After concluding the concordat with Bavaria, Pacelli was able to succeed with Prussia and Baden.…After some time in Munich, the Apostolic Nuncio's residence was transferred to Berlin."

"The Lateran Treaty of 1929 established formal relations between Italy and the Vatican. Following the example of Mussolini, Adolf Hitler initiated a concordat. This is a strictly defined legal agreement between two governments intended to preserve the freedom of the Church to teach and minister to the faithful."

On February 7, 1930, Pacelli "was appointed Secretary of State and became the archpriest of the Vatican Basilica." In this capacity, he "negotiated with the Germans to protect the rights of Catholics." Traveling widely, including an historic visit to the United States in 1936, he was seen by more people and was the most accessible Pope in the history of the papacy up to his pontificate.

In an encyclical *Mit brennender sorge*, condemning anti-Semitism, Pius XI said, "None but superficial minds could stumble into concepts of a national God, of a national religion; or attempt to lock within the frontiers of a single people, within the narrow limits of a single race, God, the Creator of the universe, King and Legislator of all nations before whose immensity they are 'as a drop of a bucket' (Isaiah XI. 15). The encyclical prepared under the direction of Cardinal Pacelli, then Secretary of State, was written in German for wider dissemination in that country. It was smuggled out of Italy, copied and distributed to parish priests to be read from all of the pulpits on Palm Sunday, March 21, 1937.... An internal German memo dated March 23, 1937, stated that the encyclical was 'almost a call to do battle against the Reich government.' The encyclical, *Mit brenneder sorge*, was confiscated, its printers were arrested and presses seized....

"Cardinal Pacelli returned to France in 1937, as Cardinal-Legate, to consecrate and dedicate the new basilica in Lisieux during a Eucharistic Congress and made another anti-Nazi statement. He again presided (May 25–30, 1938) at a Eucharistic Congress in Budapest."

"The Cardinals elected Eugenio Pacelli the 262nd Pope on his sixty-third birthday, March 2, 1939. He received sixty-one out of the sixty-two votes because he did not vote for himself, and was elected Pontiff. After serving the Church under four Popes (Leo XIII, St. Pius X, Benedict XV and Pius XI) for almost twenty years, Eugenio Pacelli took the name of Pius XII....

"Immediately after his election, Pius XII issued a call for a peace conference of European leaders. Documents show that in a last minute bid to avert bloodshed, the Pope called for a conference involving Italy, France, England, Germany and Poland. Pius XII's peace plan was based on five points: the defense of small nations, the right to life, disarmament, some new kind of League of Nations, and a plea for the moral principles of justice and love.... Pius XII then met with the German Cardinals who had been present in the recent conclave.... These meetings provided him direct proof and information that motivated the content of his first encyclical, *Summi pontificatus*. Dated October 20, 1939, this encyclical was a strong attack on totalitarianism. In it, Pius XII singled out governments, who by their deification of the state, imperiled the spirit of humanity. He spoke about restoring the foundation of human society to its origin in natural law, to its source in Christ, the only true ruler of all men and women of all nations and races.

"Pius XII reprimanded, "What age has been, for all its technical and purely civic progress, more tormented than ours by spiritual emptiness and deep-felt interior poverty?" The world had abandoned Christ's cross for another [the Swastika] which brings only death....

"On August 24, 1939, he gave each papal representative the text of a speech asking them to convey it to their respective governments. That evening he read the speech to the world [on radio]: 'The danger is imminent, but there is still time. Nothing is lost with peace; all can be lost with war. Let men return to mutual understanding! Let them begin negotiations anew, conferring with good will and with respect for reciprocal rights.' "

Mostly confined to Vatican City throughout World War II by the occupying Germans, "Pope Pius XII was almost universally regarded as a saintly man, a scholar, a man of peace, and a tower of strength." After the war, he became the first pontiff to appear on television. When he died on October 9, 1958, the future Israeli prime minister Golda Meir said, "When fearful martyrdom came to our people, the voice of the Pope was raised for its victims. The life of our times was enriched by a voice speaking out about great moral truths above the tumult of daily conflict. We mourn a great servant of peace."

The Vatican newspaper *L'osservatore Romano* described his funeral as the greatest in the long history of Rome, surpassing even that of Julius Caesar. Because the body had not been properly embalmed, it began to decompose while it lay in state in St. Peter's. As the flesh discolored, the corpse emitted such strong odors that one of the Swiss Guards fainted.

The smells and discoloration and the fact that Pius XII had been a regular exerciser and was in good health resulted in the belief by conspiracy theorists that he had been poisoned. A week before his death, he complained of gastric pain and hiccups. He struggled back into his stringent schedule, but one day as his doctor was examining him he suddenly cried in alarm, "Dio mio, non ci vedo!" (My God, I cannot see!) It was a stroke. With his vision rapidly restored, he summoned his secretary of state, Angelo Dell'Acqua, and demanded, "Why have the [papal] audiences been canceled?" He received Holy Communion and Extreme Unction from his German Jesuit secretary, Father Robert Leiber, but he looked at the thermometer when his temperature was being taken, and said, "Non é grave" (It's not bad) when he saw it read 99°. That night he drank a glass of red wine and called for a recording of Beethoven's First Symphony. At 7:30 the next morning, a second stroke left him unconscious. It took him 20 hours to die. By Vatican custom, there was no autopsy.

Later, as assertions were made that Pius XII had collaborated with the Nazis, and had done little to aid Jews, demands were raised that the Vatican open its sealed archives on Pius XII's wartime years. These requests intensified after John Paul II commenced the process to add Pius XII to the catalog of saints.

Perhaps contained in the Vatican archives are documents to shed some light on the relationship between the Holy See and the bosses of organized crime. Because La Cosa Nostra originated in Sicily and spread its tentacles to the United States and around the globe, alleged dealings between minions of the criminal underworld and the Catholic Church have been the subject of movies, such as *The Godfather* and its sequels and imitators, and almost countless books. Mystery novelist Donna Leon, best known for her subtle and enduring fictional Commissario Guido Brunetti detective series, set in Venice, once asked, "What did Italy do to deserve to have both the Vatican and the Mafia?"

In the nonfiction *The Vatican Exposed: Money, Murder and the Mafia,*

Paul L. Williams traced the origin of alleged links between Vatican and Mafia to the deal in 1929 between the Holy See and Mussolini. Through the Lateran Treaty, the Church in Rome received money, tax-free property rights, status as a sovereign state, and the protection of Mussolini's Fascist government. This resulted in the Vatican being largely insulated against interference from the Nazis during the German occupation of Italy during World War II, described by authors Mark Aarons and John Loftus in *Unholy Trinity: The Vatican, the Nazis, and Swiss Banks.*

A dramatic example of the Vatican-Mafia alliance [in 1934] involved the venerated cathedral of Naples. Its patron saint, San Gennaro (St. Januarius), Bishop of Beneventum was martyred about 305 A. D. In the Cathedral's treasure chapel were an altar of solid silver, "a silver bust believed to contain San Gennaro's head, and a reliquary with two vials of what was supposed to be his blood. [During] the feast of San Gennaro, into the Cathedral thronged clergy, civil officials, and throngs of pious Neapolitans. Bearing aloft the reliquary, a priest brought it before the silver case containing the head" and turned it upside down to exhibit a vial containing an opaque, solid mass. "After an hour of prayers the people beheld the dark mass grow soft, turn red, increase in volume, and bubble into a liquid. "Il miracolo e fatto!" (The miracle is made) cried the officiant. The choir sang a "Te Deum." The worshippers then scrambled up to the altar rail to kiss the reliquary.

This ritual usually occurred eighteen times a year. *Time* magazine reported that in 1969, "San Gennaro (St. Januarius) was dropped from the Vatican's official church calendar, along with St. Christopher and other saints whose existence was in doubt.... Among other things the Cardinal Archbishop of Naples... persuaded the congregation of the cathedral to refrain from roaring approval when the liquid bubbled.... An encyclopedia labeled the San Gennaro miracles a 'residue of paganized Christianity which the church has not managed to remove from Neapolitan usage.' That was enough to bring the blood of all Naples to a boil. San Gennaro, a newspaper editorial proclaimed, was 'not just the patron but the godfather of Naples.'... [Neapolitans] have been through it all before. In 1750 one iconoclast sought to discredit the 'Miracle' of San Gennaro as a mixture gold-affecting mercury and sulphide of mercury. In 1890 an Italian professor got results from a concoction of chocolate, water, sugar, casein, milk serum and salt. Even the Vatican's doubts did not daunt the Neapolitans. After San Gennaro lost his place on the church calendar, a fervent follower scrawled on the saint's altar in the cathedral, 'San Gennaro, don't give a damn.'"

In World War II, as American forces moved from invasion beaches at Salerno toward Naples, "the Vatican, having heard rumors that the retreating Germans... had made plans to melt down the silver of the altar of St. Januarius to pay for their occupation of southern Italy, contacted the Mafia and asked for their cooperation.... The Mafia,... also immensely religious, accepted the Vatican's proposal with pious alacrity." Because they had been cooperating with the Germans since the occupation began, they were permitted to transport" food and black-market items from Naples to Rome. "The result was that the silver of the altar was transported in Mafia trucks to the very entrance of the Vatican where it was safely deposited."

Residing in Naples at this time was American organized crime figure Vito Genovese, who had been deported from the United States in a crackdown on crime that landed Genovese's boss, Charles "Lucky" Luciano, in prison. When the U.S. Army occupied Naples, it learned that its task would be easier if it had the help of Genovese and the Neapolitan mafiosi. Michele Sindona was among the Italians who also learned that to do business in Naples in 1943, Genovese was the man to see. Michele Sindona, a Sicilian, who was the future associate of Roberto Calvi in the Vatican bank scandal, "studied law and during the war became involved in the lemon business." According to Luigi DiFonzo's biography of Sindona, "he needed to purchase a truck to transport lemons. To accomplish this, Michele Sindona needed the protection of the Mafia because it had control of the produce industry and could supply him with the documents he needed to present to the border patrols. Help came from a local bishop.... [He] got in touch with Geneovese." The result was not only a truck, but "forged papers and a safe route to do business."

Twenty years later, investigations into the Roberto Calvi murder revealed a flow of money from the Sicilian Corleone Mafia family (the real one, not the one in *The Godfather*) to Sindona and the Vatican bank. In an instance of fiction following life, in *The Godfather Part III*, Michael Corleone attempted to garner respectability and wealth through legitimate enterprise by seeking to buy the Vatican's shares in a global real estate holding company, of which one fourth was controlled by the Vatican. He negotiated a transfer of $600 million to the Vatican Bank with Archbishop Gilday, who had plunged the Holy See into debt through poor management and corruption.

While movie makers have provided entertainment by implicating a cinematic Vatican in conspiracies and historians have delved into Vatican archives in the years before World War II, the Holy See has declined to open them for the remainder of Pope Pius XII's reign (1932–58). Repeatedly urged by researchers to do so, the Vatican says some are closed for organizational reasons, but that most of the significant documentation regarding Pius XII is already available to scholars.

Pressure to make the files public has come primarily from Jewish groups and Holocaust survivors. "Until the Vatican's secret archives are declassified, Pius's record vis-a-vis Jews will continue to be shrouded and a source of controversy and contention," said ADL [Anti-Defamation League] director Abraham Foxman. "We strongly urge the Vatican to make full and complete access to the archives of this period its highest priority and call on all interested parties to assist."

Although the Vatican archives for the World War II period remain secret, other sources have revealed that the Vatican, sometimes in cooperation with the U.S. government, assisted Nazi war criminals to escape. They went from Europe and made their way to countries in South America, especially to Argentina, following a route that became known as the Rat Line.

CHAPTER 10

Spooks and Rats

Six decades after the end of World War II, a class-action lawsuit filed in federal court in San Francisco claimed that "atrocities carried out by the Nazi puppet government of Ante (Anton) Pavelic, head of the 'Catholic State of Croatia,'" had been done with the complicity of Vatican officials. "The Pavelic regime was typical of political movements that sprang up throughout Europe and had the support of so-called 'Clerical Fascism,'—an amalgam of orthodox Roman Catholic doctrine, anti-Semitism, and authoritarian politics. These groups enjoyed assistance of both the government in Italy under Mussolini, Nazi Germany's 'Ausland' department, which assisted like-minded movements" beyond Germany, and some Catholic clergy in and out of the Vatican.

"In Croatia, Pavelic's terrorists received critical funding in 1939 from Mussolini, and with the help of Archbishop A. Stepinac, to establish the Croat Separatist Movement and eventually seize power." Under Ustashi, [the secret police] a reign of terror fell "upon Jews, Orthodox Serbs who refused to convert to Catholicism, and political dissidents. Pavelic's government operated death camps, and extorted a fortune in gold and other valuables, much from Jews who were shipped to work in extermination camps in Germany. The Ustashi had the support of the Catholic Church (Archbishop Stepanic was the group's official "chaplain," he gave his blessing to the Pavelic regime), and especially the Croatian Franciscans. The San Francisco lawsuit charged that the Catholic order 'engaged in far ranging crimes including genocide [and] funding the reestablishment of the Croatian Nazi movement in South America in the 1950s.'"

The involvement of Croatian Catholics in creating an escape route for Nazis after the war was documented by American intelligence agents. Their records were preserved in the archives of the postwar Central Intelligence Agency. One of these declassified files was that of a priest, Krunoslav Stjepan Draganovic. It noted that he was born in Brcko, Bosnia. "Ordained a priest, he served in Sarajevo from 1930 to 1932. During this period he came in direct contact with Dr. Ivan Saric, the Catholic Archbishop of Bosnia." The CIA file noted that the archbishop was "perhaps the most rabid opponent of the Orthodox Serbs and the Yugoslav Royal family, which is of Serbian origin, and a vociferous champion of the Independent State of Greater Croatia (which would include all of Croatia, Dalmatia, Bosnia and Hercegovina)."

"It was under the auspices of Archbishop Saric that he [Draganovic] was sent to Rome in 1932 to attend the Instituto Orientale Ponteficio.... He obtained his doctorate in 1935 and returned to Sarajevo, where he acted as secretary to Archbishop Saric from 1935 through 1940. In February 1941 he taught Ecclesiastical History at the University of Zagreb, Croatia.

"There were conflicting reports regarding subject's [Draganovic] activities during the period from April 1941 to August 1943. According to some accounts, shortly after the Independent State of Croatia was established in April 1941 by Ante Pavelic,... via support and approval of Nazi Germany, Subject became a leading figure in the Office for Colonization,... engaged in claiming the property of Orthodox Serbs in Bosnia, Hercegovina, and Croatia" in order to distribute the property to the Ustashas (military units). "Other reports identified him as a member of a committee that forcibly converted thousands of Serbians from the Serbian Orthodox to the Roman Catholic Church. (As a result of opposition to such forcible conversions, several hundred thousand Serbs living on the territory of the Independent Croatian State reportedly died at the hands of the Ustasha.... This resulted in many Serbs, and even many Croats who were opposed to such inhuman methods, joining the Partisan guerrilla units to fight both the Germans and the Croat State.)...

"Many Serbs living outside Yugoslavia accused [Draganovic] of being personally responsible for the deaths of more than 10,000 Serbs from Croatia, killed by the Ustashas as a part of their drive to exterminate the Serbs living in Croatia."

The CIA file noted, "Subject has denied these charges, as well as the charge that he was Military Chaplain of the Domobran and Ustasha military units.... According to his own statements, Subject was instrumental in setting up a Croat-Slovene Committee for the Relief of Slovene Refugees in Zagreb in the fall of 1941, and became president of the Committee. Subject evidently became involved in mid-1943 in a feud with Eugen (aka [illegible]) Kvaternik, a major figure in the Government of Croatia and a close associate of... Ante Pavelic, the head of the Croatian State. He called Kvternik 'a madman and a lunatic.' This resulted in his 'being kicked upstairs,' which is to say, in August 1943 he went to Italy to represent the Croatian Red Cross on a mission to secure the release from camps or otherwise help Yugoslav internees. His sponsor was the... Archbishop of Zagreb. He returned to Zagreb at the end of 1943, but returned to Rome in January 1944, and was still in Italy when the Croatian State collapsed in mid-1945 at about the same time as the war ended in Europe.

"He continued to represent the Croatian Red Cross, but was also regarded as an unofficial Charge d'affairs of the Croatian State at the Vatican. Thus, when the Croatian State collapsed, he was in the ideal position to help the many Ustasha who fled Yugoslavia, and as Secretary of an organization known as the 'Confraternite Croata' in Italy he issued identity papers with false names to many Croats, primarily Ustasha who were considered to be war criminals, and is the individual most responsible for making it possible for the Ustasha to emigrate overseas, primarily to Argentina, but also to Chile, Venezuela, Australia, Canada and even the United States....

"He [Draganovic] was alleged to have provided some German Nazi war criminals with identity cards with false Croatian names, thus enabling the Nazis to emigrate from Europe and avoid standing trial in Germany.... Subject's activities in Rome were conducted from the Ecclesiastical College of San Girolamo degli Illirici,... a college sponsored by the Vatican and

used by young Croatian Catholic priests as their home in Rome while
pursuing various courses of study. It also became the sponsor of the San
Girolamo Asylum for the Ustasha and other Croat emigres in Rome....

"Subject claimed credit for helping in the release of more than 10,000
Yugoslav internees in Italy during 1943, 1944 and early 1945. In 1949, he
went to Argentina in the company of the late Ante Pavelic, but he returned to Rome shortly thereafter. In 1950 he was known to be using a
Diplomatic Passport, issued by the Vatican." "The Vatican steadfastly denied involvement in any of this, including the acquisition of Ustashi gold
and other pilfered assets."

With the end of World War II in sight, the Vatican became the hub of
traffic in counterfeit identity papers, forged travel documents, passports,
and money to assist Nazis and collaborators seeking to escape capture by
the Allies. Rome also became the start of a conduit to freedom for ex-
Nazis and known anticommunists deemed potentially valuable in a postwar confrontation that was expected to arise between a godless empire
ruled from the Kremlin in Moscow and the nations of Christendom.

To what extent Pope Pius XII and the Vatican bureaucracy were involved in the exodus of high- and low-level Nazis and other wanted men
remains sealed in the secret archives. As a result, documenting the escape
mechanism and route has been left to historians, investigative authors,
and Jewish organizations that track down war criminals. To varying de-
grees, they have all found pointers to the Vatican.

"When it became apparent that war criminals Klaus Barbie, Adolf
Eichmann, Heinrich Mueller, Franz Stangl, and a whole list of others had
escaped," the central figure in aiding them was Bishop Alois Hudal. The
Rector of the Pontificio Santa Maria dell'Anima, he had "served as Com-
missioner for the Episcopate for German-speaking Catholics in Italy, as
well as Father Confessor to Rome's large German community." Born in
Graz, Austria, in 1885, he studied theology (1904–08) and was ordained
to the priesthood In 1911, he earned a doctorate in Theology in Graz and
entered the Teutonic College of Santa Maria dell'Anima (Anima) in Rome
where he was a chaplain (1911–13) and took courses in the Old Testament

at the Biblical Institute. In World War I he served as an assistant military chaplain and published his sermons to the soldiers, *Soldatenpredigten*, in which he expressed the idea that "loyalty to the flag is loyalty to God." In 1923 he was nominated as rector of Anima. In 1930 he was appointed a consultant to the Holy Office. In 1937, he published a book titled *The Foundations of National Socialism*, in which he gave enthusiastic endorsement of Hitler. When Pope Pius XI and future Pope Pius XII (Eugenio Pacelli) expressed disapproval of the book, they broke off all contacts with Hudal. Having once been a popular and influential guest in the Vatican, he suddenly found himself in isolation in the Anima College while Mussolini became Hitler's World War II ally.

Still in the post of rector at Anima when the war ended, Hudal was suddenly thrust into a position to provide assistance to war refugees in detainment camps because of an agreement by the Allies to a request by Pope Pius XII. His Holiness had asked that a representative of the Vatican be allowed to render "normal religious assistance to Catholic prisoners as well as to exercise that mission of charity proper to the Church by bringing some comfort to those in affliction." The permission was conveyed to the Vatican by President Franklin Roosevelt's "Personal Representative to the Pope." A few weeks later, the Vatican asked that a representative be permitted to visit "the German speaking civil internees in Italy." The request named the Holy See's "Spiritual Director of the German people resident in Italy," Bishop Hudal.

Describing this as a "very peculiar request," Mark Aarons and John Loftus, authors of *Unholy Trinity*, found it "astonishing that the Holy See singled out the most notorious pro-Nazi Bishop in Rome for this extremely sensitive mission, when it was well known that these 'civilian' camps were teeming with fugitive Nazis who had discarded uniforms and were hiding among legitimate fugitives."

As the existence of a bishop in Rome who was able to aid displaced persons became known throughout refugee camps, word spread among ex-Nazis that he was sympathetic to their plight, and that Hudal had the means to facilitate their escape. Among documentation he could supply were a Vatican identity card and Red Cross papers, along with travel passes and visas.

According to Nazi hunter Simon Wiesenthal, the rat line that Bishop Hudal ran facilitated escapes for Adolf Eichmann, chief architect of the "final solution of the Jewish problem" by extermination in death camps; Franz Stangl, commandant of the Treblinka camp; Alois Brunner, deputy commandant of Sobibor; Gustav Wagner, deputy commandant of Sobibor; and Walter Rauff, a friend of Hudal, who had been an ambitious SS officer who oversaw a development program for mobile gas vans.

In Gitta Sereny's book *Into That Darkness: An Examination of Conscience*, based on seventy hours of interviews with Franz Stangl, he described "how Bishop Hudal had been expecting Stangl . . . and that he was arranging passports, an exit visa, and work permits for South America. Hudal arranged Stangl's sleeping quarters, transportation, via by car, plane, and ship and seemed to have ample money for . . . bribes and emergencies that might arise." Stangl and other "Nazi fugitives could obtain an identity card from Hudal and apply to the office of the International Red Cross for a passport. If, however, a fugitive Nazi had functioned in some capacity in the murder of Jews, then an intermediary would be sent to the Red Cross office to obtain the needed documents, because there were dozens of Jews in the office every day. . . . The danger was acute that a Jewish survivor might recognize a former concentration camp official. . . . Once fugitives had obtained new identification, they could safely venture to a soup kitchen run by the Vatican, Red Cross, or the United Nations Rehabilitation and Relief Association," then mingle with other refugees and move around Rome until time came for them to begin a circuitous route to a foreign destination, usually in South America and primarily in Argentina.

Regarding the rat line, Bishop Hudal and Father Draganovic, the official Vatican historian, Father Robert Graham, asserted, "Just because he's [Draganovic] a priest doesn't mean he represents the Vatican. It was his own operation. He's not the Vatican."

In October 1946, a Treasury Department official, Pearson Bigelow, informed the department's director of monetary research that pro-Nazi

Croatian fascists had removed valuables worth $240 million at current rates from Yugoslavia at the end of the war. The declassified document, dated October 21, 1946, said, "Approximately 200 million Swiss francs was originally held in the Vatican for safe-keeping."

Other documents established that Bigelow received reliable information from the OSS on Nazi wealth held in specific Swiss bank accounts. The Bigelow memo quoted a "reliable source in Italy" "as saying the Ustasha organization, the Nazi-installed government of Croatia during the war, had removed 350 million Swiss francs from Yugoslavian funds it had confiscated. The memo said 150 million Swiss francs were impounded by British authorities at the Austria-Swiss border and the balance was held in the Vatican, . . . and that rumors said that a considerable portion of Vatican-held money was sent to Spain and Argentina through a Vatican pipeline."

Fifty years later after a conference in London on the topic of Nazi gold that might have gone to the Vatican bank, "the Vatican's chief spokesman, Joaquin Navarro-Valls, . . . commented, "As far as gold taken by Nazis in Croatia, research in the Vatican archives confirms that there is no existence of documents relating to this, thus ruling out any supposed transaction on the part of the Holy See."

Steadfastly denying reports that it had stored money and gold for Croatian fascists after World War II, the Vatican said it had no plans to open its archives for the period, and that a search of the archives confirmed no documents existed relating to any "supposed" gold transaction "on the part of the Holy See."

"A lawsuit was filed in Federal Court in San Francisco in November 1999. The plaintiffs were concentration camp survivors of Serb, Ukrainian, Jewish, background and their relatives, as well as organizations representing over 300,000 Holocaust victims and their heirs. The plaintiffs sought an accounting and restitution of gold in the Ustasha Treasury that, according to the U.S. State Department was illicitly transferred to the Vatican, the Franciscan Order and other banks after the end of the war. Defendants included the Vatican Bank and Franciscan Order. These defendants combined to conceal assets looted by the Croatian Nazis from concentration camp victims, Serbs, Jews, Roma [gypises] and others between 1941 and 1945."

"There is one known witness to this alleged Vatican and Franciscan money laundering: former U.S. Army Counterintelligence special agent William Gowen. According to his deposition, Vatican official Fr. Krunoslav Draganovic had admitted to Gowen that he received up to ten truckloads of loot in 1946 at the Franciscan-controlled Croatian Confraternity of San Girolamo in Rome. Gowen also testified that the leader of the trea-sure convoy, Ustashe Colonel Ivan Babic, boasted to Gowen of using British uniforms and trucks to move the gold from Northern Italy to Rome. As for the Ustasha Treasury's ultimate destination, Gowen said that it could have gone nowhere but the Vatican Bank. . . .

"According to Gowen, Draganovic . . . admitted being the mastermind behind the smuggling and deposit of the Ustashe Treasury at the Vatican bank," and that Draganovic reported directly to Cardinal Giovanni Montini (the future Pope Paul VI).

In January 2006, the Israeli newspaper *Haaretz* posted an online article in which it used Gowen's testimony to accuse Cardinal Montini of in-volvement in the laundering of money for fugitive Nazi war criminals to escape by way of the "rat lines."

In a speech to a convention of the Serbian Unity Congress in Toronto in October 2000, Jonathan Levy, an attorney for twenty-eight Serbs, Jews, and others "who lost their parents and grandparents to Ustashe terror" in Croatia in World War II said the subject of a class-action lawsuit in fed-eral court in San Francisco against the Vatican Bank and the Franciscan Order was "the immense amount of property, money, gold, land, facto-ries, and other loot stolen by the Ustashe and their Independent State of Croatia between 1941 and 1945."

Levy asserted, "The Ustashe movement stole immense wealth from its victims. The genocide in Croatia and Bosnia against Serbs was not only the most barbaric of the century but had a profit motive. The war crimi-nals made sure that Serb property was seized right down to the gold teeth and wedding rings of concentration camp victims at Jasneovac. As the war was winding down, the Ustashe financial apparatus was gearing up. Top Ustashe were positioned in Rome and Switzerland, bank accounts were opened with the Swiss National Bank."

The loot included "gold, silver, jewels, and currency worth tens of millions," said Levy. "Other Ustashe reached Italy where help from the Franciscan Order was waiting in the form of safe houses, forged papers, and money." Croatian leader Ante Pavelic "struck a deal with the British, money changed hands, and a killer of 700,000 Serbs, Jews, and Gypsies became an honored guest at the Vatican, was chauffeured around Rome in a car with Vatican diplomatic license plates, and lived safely in his own compound with Ustashe guards attending to his personal security.

"The Ustashe were masters of smuggling, secret codes, and financial dealings.... Almost immediately, the Ustashe with the help of their Franciscan and Vatican sponsors,... formulated a bold plan... to fuel a mass migration of war criminals." Some historians have written that the purpose in aiding the Nazis in escaping was rooted in the desire of men such as Draganovic eventually to organize a force to resist a Soviet takeover of the Balkans.

In opposing the lawsuit, the Vatican asserted that American courts had no jurisdiction to take on the case. Agreeing to that claim, the federal district court in San Francisco dismissed the suit, but the ruling was reversed in 2005 by a decision of the Ninth Circuit Court of Appeals. In December 2007, "the district court dismissed the Vatican Bank, this time on grounds of sovereign immunity," based on the recognition of the Holy See as an independent state under the Lateran Treaty with Italy. While the plaintiffs again appealed to the Ninth Circuit Court of Appeals, the case against the Franciscans proceeded in the district court.

Although the Franciscan Order had always denied having wartime ties to the Ustashe regime in Croatia, the Order had been accused of acting as the "facilitators and middlemen in moving the contents of the Ustashe Treasury from Croatia to Austria, Italy and finally South America after the war. During the Nazi occupation of Bosnia, the Franciscans were closely involved with the Ustashe regime at a location not far from Medjugorje in Bosnia," site of a shrine where the Virgin Mary was said to appear.

In a step that dismayed victims of the Ustashe, Pope John Paul II visited Croatia in October 1998 "to announce the beatification of Cardinal Stepinac, elevating him to the last step before a declaration of sainthood. Serbs and others who recalled that Stepinac had given his blessing to Ustashe winced as 400,000 of the faithful gathered at Croatia's main shrine to the Virgin Mary to hear John Paul II hail Stepinac "as a hero" for his "resistance to Communism and his refusal to separate the Croatian church from the Vatican."

Never charged with war crimes or formally accused of funneling the purloined treasure into the Vatican bank, Father Kunoslav Draganovic, who came to be known as "the Golden Priest," spent several years after the war engaged in activities in the Balkans that ranged from dubious to nefarious and returned to Yugoslavia, where he died in 1983.

CHAPTER 11

A Fit of Madness

In a mystery with three people dead, a supposedly fake suicide note, conflicts over the crime scene and autopsies, disputed bullets, whispers about connections to Opus Dei, and charges of drug use in the Vatican that was worthy of a best-selling mystery novel or Hollywood thriller, the commander of Pope John Paul II's personal security force, the Swiss Guards, and his wife were shot to death on May 4, 1998, by a dashingly handsome young officer, who then turned the gun on himself.

The Holy See insisted that the killer was bitter at having been passed over for a medal. Another explanation was that the commander and the officer had been gay lovers. A third theory posited that the commander was killed after Vatican officials discovered that he had been a spy for the East German Stasi secret police in the 1980s. Conspiracy theorists and believers that *The Da Vinci Code* rang true, invoked the specter of a sinister plot by Opus Dei. Never in the 500-year history of the Swiss Guards had their been a whiff of scandal.

Clad in "red-yellow-and-blue tunics, plumed conquistador-style helmets, and gleaming 7-foot medieval halberds—a combined spear and battle-ax—the Swiss Guards were founded by Pope Julius II in 1506." To join the guards, a man must be a Swiss national, unmarried, a Catholic, of legitimate birth, under the age of thirty, have military training, at least five feet nine or taller, healthy, and with no bodily disfigurements. "Whoever is not eligible for military service in Switzerland is likewise refused admission into the Guards." He must present "a certificate from his home, . . . baptismal certificate, and testimonial as to character, all signed by the authorities of his parish. After a year of good conduct, the cost of the journey to Rome is refunded. . . . Those who wish to retire from the Guards may do so after giving three months' notice. After eighteen years' service each member of the Guards is entitled to a pension for life amounting to one half of his pay, after twenty years to a pension amounting to two thirds of his pay, after twenty-five years to five sixths of his pay, and after thirty years to his full pay."

Inducted to serve two-year renewable enlistments, recruits swear to lay down their life, if necessary, in defense of the supreme pontiff. They declared, "I swear I will faithfully, loyally and honorably serve the supreme pontiff [name of Pope] and his legitimate successors and also dedicate myself to them with all my strength, sacrificing if necessary also my life to defend them. I assume this same commitment with regard to the Sacred College of Cardinals whenever the See is vacant. Furthermore, I promise to the commanding captain and my other superiors, respect, fidelity and obedience. This I swear! May God and our holy patrons assist me!"

The one hundred Swiss Guards have been the only armed corps at the Vatican since Pope Paul VI dissolved three other units: the Papal Gendarmes, the Pontifical Noble Guard, and the Palatine Guard of Honor in 1970. The Swiss Guard is the remnant of the military corps that popes had at their disposal from the Middle Ages until the mid-nineteenth century, when they controlled a large part of central Italy. Swiss Guards officially assumed papal defense duties "when Pope Julius II, known as the warrior pope, recognized that he needed special protection. [H]e turned to well-known and tactically well-trained forces from Switzerland" and asked for a contingent of Swiss soldiers who would protect him and his palace. In December of that year, 150 Swiss soldiers began their march to Rome. They entered the eternal city on January 21, 1506, and set up quarters in the pope's stables. The next day, they were blessed by Julius. He bestowed on them the title "Defenders of the Church's Freedom."

Twenty-one years later, on May 6, 1527, 147 out of 189 guardsmen were killed in a defensive stance that allowed Pope Clement VII to escape attacking Spanish forces. The only blemish on the guards' record occurred in 1798. When Napoleon occupied Rome, he captured and deported Pope Pius VI, then disbanded the papal guard. Other nonpapal Swiss Guard units noted for their combat prowess were kept and integrated within the ranks of Napoleon's Grande Armée. After Hitler's troops entered Rome in World War II, Swiss Guardsmen donned gray uniforms and took up positions behind machine guns and mortars. Vastly outnumbered, they were prepared to sacrifice their lives for Pius XII, but by Hitler's order, the Germans did not move against the Vatican.

"Today a pope's temporal authority extends over just the 108-acre enclave of Vatican City.... The Swiss Guards now perform ceremonial functions but also stand guard duty outside the papal apartments and at the Vatican's four main entrances. Guards in plain clothes accompany the pope on his travels...and cooperate with other church security forces and police...to ensure the pope's protection. These days, the guards carry tear gas for crowd control and train weekly with machine pistols and handguns at an Italian army firing range." The force usually consists of four officers, twenty-three noncommissioned officers, seventy halberdiers (lance carriers), two drummers, and a chaplain, all with an equivalent Italian army rank. Although they are fully trained and equipped in modern weaponry and tactics, they also receive instructions in using the sword and halberd.

"Their official dress uniform was altered in 1915. It is a jumpsuit which has a distinctly Renaissance appearance. A popular misconception is that these dress uniforms were designed by Michelangelo. The working uniform is more functional, consisting of blue coveralls and black beret. Both dress and working uniforms are worn by the Guardsmen when on duty in Vatican City."

"All the officers carry out guard duties every day as well as on occasions such as Masses, audiences, and receptions.... The officers and the Sergeant Major generally wear civilian clothes when on duty.... The chaplain has the equivalent title of an army lieutenant colonel." "The Guard quarters consist of two narrow parallel buildings which with the Sistine Palace and the Torrione di Niccolò V form two courts. The inner court is adjacent to the palace, in the other is a gate leading directly to the city." "The corps has its own chapel, SS Martino e Sebastiano, built by Pius V in 1568."

A member of the Swiss Guard on May 4, 1989, Jacques-Antoine Fierz, wrote in *Newsweek* magazine, "It takes a special sort of man to leave behind the tranquil life of the Swiss cantons for a barracks in a foreign land. After all, it's not a job full of material rewards. The hours are long—sixty or seventy a week when there are no extraordinary duties. The pay is merely 1.8 million lire ($1,000) a month—far less than an Italian soldier would earn. It's not easy to stand like a statue for many hours holding a heavy pike. And we're all normal guys who carry on like all other young men our age. We go out with friends in the neighborhood, have a few drinks at a pub with our comrades and swap work stories. Some of us even have girlfriends. To be a soldier of the pope does not imply a vow of celibacy, and it's not rare for a Guardsman to come home with a wife he met in Rome. But there is very little free time, and bed check is at midnight every day."

At age forty-three, Colonel Alois Estermann was "an 18-year veteran of the Swiss Guard Corps, who distinguished himself by shielding the pope's body with his own during the assassination attempt in St. Peter's Square on May 13, 1981."

Only inches away from John Paul II when Mehmet Ali Agca attempted to assassinate him, Estermann had become close to the pontiff and accompanied him on more than thirty foreign trips and on John Paul's annual mountain-climbing retreats. "Described by his men as a straight-arrow professional soldier, Estermann had just achieved his life's ambition at noon" on May 4, 1998, when John Paul II consecrated him in the post of commander of the Swiss Guard detachment. His forty-nine-year-old wife, Gladys Meza Romero, "was a striking ex-model from Venezuela who worked in the library of Venezuela's embassy. Married since 1983, they had no children." Everyone in the Swiss Guard and the Vatican hierarchy considered them to be a model couple.

Since the retirement of his predecessor, Roland Buchs, "Estermann had waited six months for the appointment as commander of the Guard.... The post traditionally goes to a Swiss nobleman, and Estermann was a commoner. But the tradition had become difficult to maintain, especially for a job that paid about $30,000 a year." Estermann was only the fourth nonaristocrat chosen to lead the guards in their nearly five centuries of existence."

"Finishing his second two-year enlistment in the Guard," twenty-three-year-old Vice Corporal Cedric Tornay, "who was on his second Italian fiancée, had been cited five times for failing to make bed check at midnight and was criticized for drinking too much and swearing.... Estermann had given Tornay a written reprimand. He passed him over for awards that were to be distributed ... in an annual ceremony at which [Alois Estermann] was to be publicly installed as commander.

Sometime on May 4, 1989, Tornay wrote a letter to his mother that read, "Mama, I hope you will forgive me, for it is they who made me to do what I have done. This year I should have received the decoration (la "Benemerenti") but the Lieutenant-Colonel refused to give it to me. After 3 years, 6 months and 6 days spent here putting up with all kinds of injustices, he refused to give me the only thing I wanted. I owe this duty to all the guards as well as to the Catholic Church. I took an oath to give my life for the Pope and that is what I am doing. Forgive me for leaving you all alone but my duty calls me. Tell Sarah, Melissa and Papa that I love you. Cedrich."

Around 7:20 P.M. the letter was entrusted to a colleague.

An hour later, Tornay called a Swiss priest he had known since childhood. He got the priest's voice mail. "Padre Ivano, please call me back," Tornay said with an urgent tone. "It's an emergency."

Wearing jeans and black leather jacket, he walked in the rain across a courtyard, passed under the lighted apartment of Pope John Paul II, and reached the barracks of the Swiss Guard next to the Palace.

A nun heard him going hurriedly up the stairs, looked, but saw nothing.

Tornay entered Estermann's apartment building at about nine o'clock. "Estermann was speaking to a priest friend by telephone when shots rang out.

"By 9:05 P.M., all three people [in the apartment] were dead."

Within minutes of being urgently summoned to the scene by a neighbor, the papal spokesman, Joaquin Navarro-Valls, sealed the Estermanns' apartment. No one was allowed to enter it, including the Italian police. Within three hours, Navarro-Valls issued this statement on behalf of the Vatican: "The Captain Commander of the Pontifical Swiss Guard, Colonel Alois Estermann, was found dead in his home together with his wife, Gladys Meza Romero, and Vice Corporal Cedric Tornay. The bodies were discovered shortly after 9 p.m. by a neighbor from the apartment next door who was attracted by loud noises. From a first investigation it is possible to affirm that all three were killed by a firearm. Under the body of the vice corporal his regulation weapon was found. The information which has emerged up to this point allows for the theory of a 'fit of madness' by Vice Corporal Tornay."

Noting that Holy See officials said it was the first murder in the Vatican in 150 years, *Newsweek* magazine reported the Vatican's explanation, but cited doubts. For a case that was supposed to be open and shut, it said, "the Vatican could not convince everyone that it had told the whole tragic story.

"The Vatican will not give us the full truth about my brother's death," said Tornay's sister, Melinda.

The soldier's mother, Mugette Baudet, said she spoke to her son by telephone the afternoon before the killings. "He was not angry or bitter," she said. "If he had been upset, it was not enough to kill anyone."

A Berlin tabloid quoted anonymous sources who claimed that Estermann once supplemented his meager salary by selling Vatican secrets to the Stasi, the notorious East German secret police. Italian columnists speculated about a love triangle gone sour. "The relationship could not be other than one of a homosexual nature," Ida Magli, a prominent anthropologist, told the Roman daily *Il Messaggero*.

Frank Grillini, head of Arcigay, Italy's leading gay organization,

·claimed, "The Holy See wanted to close a case in a hurry, perhaps out of a need to hide a sad, worrisome truth. It's been known for years that many of the Swiss Guards are homosexuals. These men are isolated and shut away, which is why we see these gay tendencies in the Swiss Guard and in all Vatican institutions."

The Vatican dismissed the espionage charge as beneath contempt and took pains to deny rumors of a sexual motive for the killings.

"The barracks is a ghetto," said Hugues de Wurstemberg, a former Guard who lived in Belgium. "It's like a stew in a pressure cooker. Lots of alcohol, stories of theft, rumors of homosexuality, desertions, rancor."

"It's a hard life, and these are young guys," said Mario Biasetti, an American filmmaker who spent two years with the Guards to produce a documentary called *Soldiers of the Pope*. "But they're also very serious about their duties, and they're all volunteers. If they don't like it, they only have two years to go."

"The triple homicide was the latest in a disturbing series of violent episodes connected to St. Peter's," *Newsweek* recorded. "[In] January, the body of Enrico Sini Luzi, a nobleman who served as a Gentleman of the Pope, was found in his elegant apartment near the Vatican. He was bludgeoned to death with an antique chandelier. Until his death, Luzi had served as a papal usher, even though he had been arrested years before for having sex in a public bathroom, allegedly with a priest. A male prostitute was charged with Luzi's murder. Shortly afterward, a gay man from Sicily set himself on fire in St. Peter's Square to protest the Catholic Church's position on homosexuality.

"In the [previous] year, three plots had been uncovered to put bombs in the pope's path.... When CIA Director George Tenet visited Rome late [in 1997], Western diplomatic sources said, it was to pay a call on the Vatican's secretary of State, Cardinal Angelo Sodano, to warn of terrorists who might be targeting the pontiff....

"Moving quickly to try to repair any damage to morale" in the Guards after the Estermann murders, "the Vatican brought back the popular Buchs as commander. But from outside the walls of the papal state, there were suggestions that the Swiss Guard should be disarmed again, or even replaced by a modern police force." Countering this idea, Swiss Cardinal Amedee Grab said, 'Without the Swiss Guard, or with a disarmed Swiss Guard, it would be impossible to ensure the security of the pope.'

"Estermann and his wife were given a funeral in St. Peter's Basilica that was concelebrated by 16 cardinals and 30 bishops. All available Guardsmen turned out, standing composed and impassive through the mass. Before the service, Pope John Paul II prayed at all three caskets, which were displayed, side by side, for viewing. Vatican officials gave Tornay a proper funeral, despite the Church's condemnation of suicide. A crowd of his Roman friends gathered at the parish church of Santa Ana, within Vatican walls. The Swiss Guards also turned out, with many of them weeping openly, as they had not done for Estermann. The Guardsmen's band played 'I Had a Good Comrade.'"

In its May 18, 1998, issue, *Newsweek* presented an account of life in the Swiss Guards by Jacques-Antoine Fierz. A member from 1992 to 1995, he had returned "to Rome to join annual ceremonies known as the Swearing In, in which the Swiss Guards...renew their allegiances. Instead, he attended a funeral."

"We are, it has been said, the pope's calling cards, the Vatican's finest," he said, "And here were three dead among us, all three absurd deaths—a loss that has profoundly wounded us all. It is only invidious bad-mouthers who speak ill of the Swiss Guard, and among those I count the ones who are floating these provocative theories that Cedric Tornay and Estermann were homosexuals. It is impossible, inconceivable. We live and work in such close quarters that we would surely have known if anything like that went on. It didn't. Those who say otherwise are jealous of the prestige the Swiss Guard has gained throughout its history....

"The Swiss who become the pope's soldiers are simply young men with high enough ideals to take on huge responsibilities, those who want to dedicate their lives to the service of one man and all that he represents.

"I don't know a single Guard who really minded the hours or the duties," he said. "The great majority of us feel a very strong affinity for the church, the pontiff and the military life, and the discipline and the adventure it represents. And it's not bad to improve your language skills, or to live in one of the most beautiful cities in the world. Also, I can't deny the fascination of being part of the oldest continually serving army in the world. And I admit that it's something else to be able to dress up in those elegantly colored uniforms, however out of fashion they may now seem. If I sound enthusiastic, it's because I remember my time at the Vatican very positively, especially the spirit of camaraderie. That's what makes this tragedy so sadly incomprehensible. I talked to a lot of the Guards after the murders, and they all said the same thing—it was so senseless, so impossible to imagine. I agree. Estermann had been my lieutenant colonel. He had wonderful human qualities, was an exemplary believer and a very correct officer. His wife, Gladys, was pleasant and well educated. I remember Cedric Tornay as very kindly.... This was an act of a madman, not of Tornay the Guard."

"After a nine-month internal inquiry, the text of which remained secret, the Vatican repeated the claim that Tornay acted in a fit of madness, saying traces of cannabis were found in Tornay's urine, and a cyst 'the size of a pigeon's egg' in his head, helped explain the 'madness.'"

A year after the killings, a group of disaffected priests within the Vatican claimed that Estermann was the victim of a Vatican power struggle. Calling themselves "the disciples of truth," they claimed that evidence had been tampered with in order to fit the hypothesis that the killing was the result of a moment of madness on the part of Tornay. In a book titled *Blood Lies in the Vatican*, they said that the struggle was between the secretive, traditionalist Catholic movement Opus Dei and a Masonic power faction among the Curia for control of the Swiss Guard.

"'In the Vatican, there are those who maintain that Vice Corporal Tornay was attacked after coming off duty and dragged into a cellar,' the book said. Tornay was then 'suicided' with a silenced 7mm pistol, and his duty revolver used to kill the Estermanns in their Vatican apartment. His body was dumped in the Estermann's flat so that the triple killing would appear to be a murder-suicide."

The book alleged that "Estermann and his wife...were actively engaged in secret international financial deals for the benefit of Opus Dei."

Those who discerned a conspiracy asserted that a Vatican inquiry had been rigged, as was the case in the assassination of John Paul I twenty years earlier, and in the murder of Roberto Calvi. It was alleged that a "veritable piece of stagecraft was orchestrated at midnight, [in which] an ambulance from the Vatican's Health Assistance Fund...pretended to transport 'three bodies' to the Gemelli Polyclinic Hospital, when...the three victims were actually placed on stretchers which halberdiers transported to the Vatican morgue next to Saint Anne's Church. It was imperative to prevent an autopsy taking place outside the Vatican or on the premises of the Health Assistance Fund. The three corpses were therefore taken away without any of the precautions routinely used in criminal investigations...and placed in the corridor of the morgue, then covered with sheets."

The conspiracy theorists said "the inquiry was entrusted to the only judge in the Vatican State, Gianluigi Marrone. He decided that the autopsy would be carried out the following day, within the Vatican, by forensic pathologists Pietro Fucci and Giovanni Arcudi, who could be trusted to do what was necessary."

In 2003, Anglo-French writer John Follain drew several startling conclusions in his book, *City of Secrets: The Startling Truth Behind the Vatican Murders.* Author of books on the Mafia and Carlos the Jackal, Follain asserted that the official explanation for the deaths of Estermann, his wife, and Tornay was a "hastily cobbled cover-up" concerning a papal protective force in which "homosexuality was common, with as many as one quarter of the Swiss Guards gay, morale low, and fundamental reform desperately needed." Follain agreed that "Tornay was the murderer, but he said he discovered a morass of abuse, discrimination and misery behind the young guard's desperate act. 'The decision not to award Tornay the medal was the trigger,' he said. 'But it was not an act of madness: it was premeditated.'

"Other grievances had been simmering in Swiss-French Tornay. He suffered prejudice and discrimination by the majority Swiss-Germans in the force. He believed the Swiss Guard was amateurish and not up to the duty of protecting the Pope, and had urged reform of the body. Nobody was listening. He had also had a homosexual affair with Estermann, who had hurt him by moving on to other lovers."

Tornay's mother stated that his letter to her was a forgery by someone who knew him well. She noted that it was addressed to the name "Chamorel," but her son always used her maiden name, Baudat. Graphologists from Switzerland attested that Tornay had not written the letter. She also said "an independent autopsy in Lausanne established that a 7mm bullet killed her son—not a 9.4mm caliber bullet from a Stig 75 gun, as claimed in the Vatican's investigation. She claims the autopsy suggested her son was drugged, then shot and his body positioned in Estermann's flat to make it seem that he killed the couple before shooting himself."

In 2005, "high-profile French lawyer Jacques Vergès and his colleague, Luc Brossollet, acting for Tornay's mother, said that they would file a murder claim" in Switzerland because Tornay was Swiss. They said they had "faced years of stubborn deafness from the Vatican."

On May 7, 2006, "Benedict XVI thanked the Swiss Guards for 500 years of service and invited them to continue their mission with 'courage and fidelity.'" The Pope said this during a Mass commemorating the 500th anniversary of the arrival in Rome "of the first 150 Swiss Guards, requested by Pope Julius II. Also remembered were the 147 Swiss Guards killed while defending Pope Clement VII during the sacking of Rome on May 6, 1527. In his homily delivered in Italian, French and German, ... The Holy Father said that his purpose for the meeting was to render honor to the Swiss Guard corps.

"'For all, to be a Swiss Guard means to adhere without reservations to Christ and his Church, to be ready to give his life,' he said. 'The effective service may finish, but within one is always a Swiss Guard.'"

He said the Swiss Guard had always been constant, even in 1970 when Paul VI dissolved all the other military corps of the Vatican but the Guard.

Two years after this accolade, Benedict stripped the Swiss Guard of its sole role in papal protection. Some of the duties were handed to the Holy See's second, and larger, protection service, the Vatican Gendarmerie.

When the commander of the Guard, Elmar Theodor Maeder, quit in protest, Benedict appointed Daniel Rudolf Anrig, a senior police officer from the Swiss canton of Glarus and a former lecturer in civil and church law at Freiburg University. The Rome newspaper, *Il Messaggero*, suggested that "despite the long-standing rivalry between the two forces, Anrig and [Domenico] Giani," head of the 180 gendarmes and a former officer in the Guardia di Finanza, the Italian financial police, "would find cooperation because they were 'of a similar age,' thanks to Pope Benedict's policy of promoting younger men and women."

For the first time in five hundred years, the Swiss Guard that Cedric Tornay wished to reform was no longer the sole protector of a Pope's physical safety.

CHAPTER 12

Vatican Espionage

A few days after Cedric Tornay murdered the commander of the Swiss Guard, Italian newspapers bristled with articles based on mere rumors that Colonel Alois Estermann had been a spy for Communist East Germany. No evidence was provided to support the claim, but the annals of the Vatican contain ample proof that cloak-and-dagger business was carried out against and for the Holy See.

"For five centuries, the Vatican has used a secret spy service, called the Holy Alliance, or later, the Entity. Forty popes have relied on it to carry out their policies. They have played hitherto a role in confronting" Church schisms, revolutions, dictators, civil wars and world wars, assassinations and kidnappings. According to historian Eric Frattini, "the Entity was involved in killings of monarchs, poisonings of diplomats, financing of South American dictators, protection of war criminals, the laundering of Mafia money, manipulation of financial markets, provocation of bank failures, and financing of arms sales to combatants even as their wars were condemned, all in the name of God." The Entity's motto was "With the Cross and the Sword."

Espionage expert David Alvarez, professor of politics at Saint Mary's College of California, author of *Nothing Sacred: Nazi Espionage Against the Vatican, 1939–1945* and the later *Spies in the Vatican: Espionage & Intrigue from Napoleon to the Holocaust*, in collaboration with Robert Graham, S. J., investigated "espionage in the pontificates of eleven popes, [starting] with Pius VI who died in 1799 as a prisoner of the French during the French

Revolution [and concluding] with Pius XII.... The period from the Congress of Vienna in 1814 to the end of the Papal States in 1870 was the high point of papal intelligence 'to navigate between the rocks of internal revolution and shoals of foreign intervention and aggression.' Finally, with the disappearance of the Papal States intelligence capabilities of the papacy largely vanished."

At the beginning of the twentieth century, a new domestic intelligence unit of Monsignor Umberto Benigni was aimed at "modernist" liberal Catholics' reform ideas. "His organization for propaganda and disinformation was short-lived." From the beginning of World War I in 1914 to the end of the Second World War, the secular world experienced an intelligence revolution which "completely bypassed the Papacy." Between the wars, a "secret mission of Bishop Michael d'Herbigny in 1926 to re-establish a Catholic Church organization in the Soviet Union failed. His covert operation was compromised from its very beginning."

In the Vatican review *La Civiltá Cattolica* (*The Catholic Civilization*), U.S. Jesuit Robert A. Graham wrote in 1970 that between 1939 and 1945, the "Nazis distrusted the Vatican and flooded Rome with bogus priests and lay spies in an effort to discover whether it was plotting against them. The Germans were astute enough to fathom one thing about Catholicism: it abounds in rumor and thrives on hearsay. 'In place of this river of unreliable information, we need authentic news which is really important,' read a 1943 report... [to] Berlin from Ernst von Weizsacker, who as Ambassador to the Holy See also directed a German spy network" in an effort to pierce the Vatican's inner circles.

"Assigned to ferret out authentic news for the Germans was an apostate priest named Georg Elling, who came to Rome ostensibly to study the life of St. Francis of Assisi. What really interested him was the movements of the Allied ambassadors at the Vatican. Other spies tapped telephones, monitored Vatican Radio transmissions and intercepted cables. [The German aviation ministry] cracked the code by which Rome communicated with Archbishop Cesare Orsenigo, its apostolic nuncio in Berlin."

According to Graham, "the Germans were principally interested in... what they referred to as Ostpolitik des Vatikans (Eastern European political policy)." Despite the Church's well-known hostility to the Soviet Union's Communism, Hitler was obsessed with the idea that the Vatican and the Kremlin would form an alliance. This alarm heightened in 1942 when Pope Pius VII "ordered two monsignors to study Russian."...

"Nazi leaders like Martin Bormann and Reinhard ("The Hangman") Heydrich were also interested in what Heydrich called 'political Catholicism.' Certain that the Church was attempting to establish a political alternative to the Nazi Party in Germany, they monitored all contacts between Rome and the German bishops for signs of scheming."

After researching "U.S., German and Vatican archives," Graham concluded that Pope Pius XII was "vaguely aware of what was happening. To thwart the Germans, Pius depended on the loyalty of those around him, rather than on counterespionage.... Those close to the Pope, Graham found, kept their secrets... 'because they are bound by the faith.' As a result, the Germans learned little" from at least five Nazi agencies with espionage agents in Rome.

Even more obsessed with the Pope as a political nemesis and threat were the suspicious men who ran the Soviet Union's spy agency.

In 2007, former Romanian lieutenant general Ion Mihai Pacepa wrote in an article for *National Review Online* that in 1960 the Kremlin of Nikita Khrushchev sought to discredit the papacy by showing that Pope Pius XII collaborated with the Nazis. To accomplish this, said Pacepa, "the KGB needed some original Vatican documents, even ones only remotely connected with Pius XII, which its *dezinformatsiya* experts could slightly modify and project in the 'proper light' to prove the Pope's 'true colors.' The difficulty was that the KGB had no access to the Vatican archives."

The Soviets turned to the Romanian foreign intelligence service (DIE). "The new chief of the Soviet foreign intelligence service, General Aleksandr Sakharovsky, had created the DIE in 1949 and had... been its chief Soviet adviser, he knew that the DIE was in an excellent position to contact the Vatican and obtain approval to search its archives."

Pacepa wrote, "In 1959, when I had been assigned to West Germany in the cover position as deputy chief of the Romanian Mission, I had conducted a 'spy swap' under which two DIE officers (Colonel Gheorghe

Horobet and Major Nicolae Ciuciulin), who had been caught red-handed in West Germany, had been exchanged for Roman Catholic bishop Augustin Pacha, who had been jailed by the KGB on a spurious charge of espionage and was finally returned to the Vatican via West Germany."

In the KGB plan, code-named "Seat-12," Pacepa became its Romanian point man. "To facilitate [his task], Sakharovsky authorized him to [falsely] inform the Vatican that Romania was ready to restore its severed relations with the Holy See, in exchange for access to its archives and a one-billion-dollar, interest-free loan for twenty-five years. (Romania's relations with the Vatican had been severed in 1951, when Moscow accused the Vatican's *nunciatura* in Romania of being an undercover CIA front and closed its offices. The *nunciatura* buildings in Bucharest had been turned over to the DIE.)" Pacepa was to say that "access to the Papal archives... was needed in order to find historical roots that would help the Romanian government justify its change of heart toward the Holy See. The billion [dollar loan was]... to make Romania's turnabout more plausible. 'If there's one thing those monks understand, it's money,' Sakharovsky remarked."

A month after receiving the KGB's instructions, Pacepa had his "first contact with a Vatican representative. For secrecy reasons the meeting—and most of the ones that followed—took place at a hotel in Geneva, Switzerland. [Pacepa] was introduced to an 'influential member of the diplomatic corps' who, he was told, had begun his career working in the Vatican archives. His name was Monsignor Agostino Casaroli.... This Monsignor gave access to the Vatican archives, and soon three young DIE undercover officers posing as Romanian priests were digging around in the papal archives. Casaroli also agreed 'in principle' to Bucharest's demand for the interest free loan, but said the Vatican wished to place certain conditions on it...."

"[From] 1960 to 1962, the DIE succeeded in pilfering hundreds of documents connected in any way with Pope Pius XII from Vatican Archives and the Apostolic Library. Everything was immediately sent to the KGB via special courier. In actual fact, no incriminating material against the pontiff ever turned up in all those secretly photographed documents.

Mostly they were copies of personal letters and transcripts of meetings and speeches, couched in routine diplomatic language."

Using this material, according to Pacepa, the KGB developed a play in which Pope Pius XII was depicted cooperating with the Nazis, with full knowledge of the program for exterminating Jews. With the playwright cited as Rolf Hochhuth, the title in German was *Der Stellvertreter. Ein christliches Trauerspiel (The Deputy, a Christian Tragedy)*. The published text of the eight-hour drama was accompanied by "historical documentation."

In a newspaper article published in Germany in 1963, Hochhuth defended his portrayal of Pius XII. "The facts are there," he said, "forty crowded pages of documentation in the appendix to my play."

In a radio interview given in New York in 1964, when *The Deputy* opened there, Hochhuth said, "I considered it necessary to add to the play a historical appendix, fifty to eighty pages (depending on the size of the print)."

Pacepa claimed that "before writing *The Deputy*, Hochhuth, who did not have a high school diploma, was working in various inconspicuous capacities for the Bertelsmann publishing house. In interviews he claimed that in 1959 he took a leave of absence from his job and went to Rome, where he spent three months talking to people and then writing the first draft of the play, and where he posed 'a series of questions' to one bishop whose name he refused to reveal."

Pacepa noted, "At about that same time I used to visit the Vatican fairly regularly as an accredited messenger from a head of state, and I was never able to get any talkative bishop off into a corner with me, and it was not for lack of trying. The DIE illegal officers that we infiltrated into the Vatican also encountered almost insurmountable difficulties in penetrating the Vatican secret archives, even though they had airtight cover as priests."

During its first ten years of life, "*The Deputy* generated a flurry of books and articles, some accusing and some defending the pontiff. Some went so far as to lay the blame for Auschwitz concentration camp atrocities on the Pope's shoulders," and some books attacked Hochhuth's arguments.

When evidence was presented by researchers in the 1970s that Hitler had been plotting against Pius XII, including a plan to kidnap him, KGB chief Yuri Andropov conceded to Pacepa that "had we known then what we know today," the KGB would never have gone after Pius XII.

A decade later, as described in chapter 7, the KGB turned to its puppet spy service in Bulgaria in an effort to silence Pope John Paul II as he expressed support for Poland's Solidarity movement.

Upon the death of John Paul II, keepers of Vatican secrets found themselves forced to guard against journalistic spies intent upon eavesdropping on the College of Cardinals as the princes of the Church met to elect John Paul II's successor.

The Associated Press reported, "Computer hackers, electronic bugs and supersensitive microphones threaten to pierce the Vatican's thick walls next week when cardinals gather in the Sistine Chapel to name a papal successor."

Confident it could protect the centuries-old tradition of secrecy that surrounds the gathering, one official said, "It's not as if it's the first conclave we've handled."

"Vatican security refused to discuss the details of any anti-bugging measures to be used during the conclave. But Giuseppe Mazzullo, a private detective and retired Rome policeman whose former unit worked closely with the Vatican in the past, said the Holy See would reinforce its own experts with Italian police and private security contractors."

"The security is very strict," Mazzullo said. "For people to steal information, it's very, very difficult, if not impossible."

CHAPTER 13

The Devil, You Say

"Thank God we have a Pope who has decided to confront the devil head-on."

So said Father Gabriele Amorth, the official exorcist of the Rome diocese, when he heard a report in 2007 that Pope Benedict XIV would soon undertake a new campaign to combat demonic possession.

An expert on the subject and author of a popular book on exorcism and demonic possession, age seventy-five and a priest for fifty years, Amorth spoke as "the undisputed leader of Rome's six exorcists...and honorary president-for-life of the International Association of Exorcists."

"I speak with the Devil every day," he said to an interviewer while "grinning like a benevolent gargoyle. 'I talk to him in Latin. He answers in Italian. I have been wrestling with him, day in day out, for fourteen years.'"

Born in 1925 in "Modena, northern Italy, the son and grandson of lawyers," he joined the Italian resistance as a teenager in World War II. "Immediately after the war, he became a member of Italy's fledgling Christian Democratic Party. Giulio Andreotti was president of the Young Christian Democrats, Amorth was his deputy. Andreotti went into politics and was seven times prime minister. Amorth, having studied law at university, went into the Church."

"From the age of fifteen," he recalled, "I knew it was my true vocation. My speciality was the Madonna. For many years I edited the magazine

Madre di Deo (*Mother of God*). . . . I knew nothing of exorcism—I had given it no thought—until June 6, 1986, when Cardinal Poletti, the then Vicar of Rome, asked to see me. There was a famous exorcist in Rome then, the only one, Father Candido, but he was not well, and Cardinal Poletti told me I was to be his assistant. I learnt everything from Father Candido. He was my great master. Quickly I realized how much work there was to be done and how few exorcists there were to do it. From that day, I dropped everything and dedicated myself entirely to exorcism."

In 2008, he said to the website Petrus that a "new Vatican document would call for the designation of exorcists in every Catholic diocese around the world. . . . But Father Federico Lombardi, the director of the Vatican press office, flatly denied the Petrus report. The papal spokesman said, 'Pope Benedict XVI has no intention of ordering local bishops to bring in garrisons of exorcists to fight demonic possession.' "

Taking note of these conflicting statements, the Catholic World News service reported, "The topic of exorcism commands considerable public interest in Italy, and Father Amorth has frequently generated attention with warnings about the unchecked spread of diabolical influence. In a new course on the topic, being offered by Rome's pontifical university Regina Apostolorum, Father Paolo Scarafoni warned that while Satanic cults were making inroads in society, and the influence of the devil was real, he reported that most suspected cases of demonic possession could be explained by other factors."

On January 26, 1999, the Prefect of the Vatican's Congregation for Divine Worship and the Discipline of the Sacraments, Cardinal Jorge Arturo Medina Estevez, had revealed a revised Roman Catholic ritual for driving out demons. Although he stressed that few people were actually possessed by demons, and that "only one in every 5,000 reported cases is an actual demonic possession," John Paul II reaffirmed that the Devil exists and was at work in the world.

According to the *New York Times*, Pope John Paul II acted "in an apparent effort to placate liberal Catholics embarrassed by a practice that seems to echo medieval superstition" by urging those performing exorcisms to "take pains to distinguish between possessed people and others suffering from forms of mental or psychological illness." The *Times* noted that exorcism is the "ancient practice of driving the Devil from people believed to be possessed. It remains a source of theological debate and in recent years, despite its renewed popularity in the United States and elsewhere, the Church has sought to play down its significance without shaking the foundations of belief in a personal source of evil in the world."

"In a Latin text titled, *De Exorcismis et Supplicationibus Quibusdam* (*Of Exorcisms and Certain Supplications*), the Vatican cautioned that exorcists "first of all, must not consider people to be vexed by demons who are suffering above all from some psychic illness.". . .

"By issuing the text, which replaced a 1614 version, the Vatican reaffirmed the existence of the Devil. . . . The eighty-four-page document, which Pope John Paul II approved before he departed for a visit to North America, contained the prayers and rites for driving out devils, but also for cleansing places and things of demonic influence. . . .

"Cardinal Medina Estevez . . . said genuine possession could be recognized by various criteria, including the use of unknown languages, extraordinary strength and the disclosure of hidden occurrences or events. He also mentioned a 'vehement aversion to God, the Blessed Virgin, the saints, the cross and sacred images.' [He] acknowledged that many modern Catholics no longer believed in the Devil, but he called this a 'serious fault in religious education,' adding that the existence of the Devil 'belongs to Catholic faith and doctrine.

"'Exorcism is based on the faith of the Church,' said Estevez, 'which holds that Satan and other evil spirits exist and that their activity consists in diverting human beings from the way of salvation. Catholic doctrine teaches us that the demons are angels who have fallen because of sin, that they are spiritual beings of great intelligence and power, but I would like to stress that the evil influence of the devil and his followers is usually exercised through deceit and confusion. Just as Jesus is the Truth, so the Devil is the liar par excellence. He deceives human beings by making them believe that happiness is found in money, power or carnal desire. He deceives them into thinking that they do not need God, that grace and salvation are unnecessary. He even deceives them by diminishing the sense

of sin or even suppressing it altogether, replacing God's law as the crite-
rion of morality with the habits or conventions of the majority.'"

The Roman Catholic catechism states that "Jesus performed exorcisms
and from him the Church has received the power and office of exorcizing.
In a simple form, exorcism is performed at the celebration of Baptism.
The solemn exorcism, called 'a major exorcism,' can be performed only
by a priest and with the permission of the bishop. The priest must pro-
ceed with prudence, strictly observing the rules established by the Church.
Exorcism is directed at the expulsion of demons or to the liberation from
demonic possession 'through the spiritual authority which Jesus entrusted
to his Church.'"

In Ephesians 6: 12–13, St. Paul said. "Our wrestling is not against flesh
and blood; but against principalities and power, against the rulers of the
world of this darkness, against the spirits of wickedness in the high places.
Therefore take unto you the armor of God, that you may be able to resist
in the evil day, and to stand in all things perfect."

In a book published in 2008, *The Sistine Secrets*, authors Benjamin Blech,
a rabbi, and Roy Doliner wrote that when Michelangelo began work on
the Sistine Chapel ceiling he embedded messages of "brotherhood, toler-
ance, and freethinking" in his painting to encourage "fellow travelers" to
challenge the "repressive" Church of his time. They wrote, "Driven by
the truths he had come to recognize during his years of study in private
nontraditional schooling in Florence, truths rooted in his involvement
with Judaic texts as well as Kabbalistic training that conflicted with approved Christian doctrine, Michelangelo needed to find a way to let view-
ers discern what he truly believed. He could not allow the Church to
forever silence his soul. And what the Church would not permit him to
communicate openly, he ingeniously found a way to convey to those dili-
gent enough to learn his secret language."

Blech and Doliner contended that what "Michelangelo meant in the
angelic representations was to mock his papal patron...[by sneaking
Jewish symbols that at the time were] unorthodox heresies into his ostensibly pious portrayals...to fulfill his lifelong ambition to bridge the wis-

dom of science with the strictures of faith. The authors claimed to have unearthed secrets that were hidden in plain sight for centuries." "The book's starting point was that there is not one Christian figure or image out of the hundreds of figures in the entire ceiling of the Papal chapel. They asserted that in defiance of Pope Julius III, Michelangelo...changed the original Christian design to an overwhelmingly Judaic subject. [Vatican experts held that] the ceiling emphasized that the choice of subjects simply presented the ancestors of Jesus and theological antecedents to the triumph of Christianity."

Elected pope in 1550, Julius III looted the papal coffers to renovate his own mansion in Rome. The Villa Giula, as it is known, became the full-time residence of Julius III and the pope oversaw the construction. "Julius III appointed a teenage boy, [Innocenzo Ciocchi Del Monte,] as his first cardinal. Julius had picked up Innocenzo on the streets of Parma when Innocenzo was aged fifteen and a beggar boy. The Venetian ambassador reported that Innocenzo slept with the pope (Pope Julius III). Julius allowed Innocenzo to become richer than the Medicis. Reportedly, Julius made love with cardinals, pages, and young men he fancied...."

"Other famous gay popes included, reportedly, Pope Benedict IX, Pope John XII, Pope Sixtus IV, and Pope Leo X." Writing in1525, Francesco Guicciardini (1483–1540) recorded that at the beginning of Leo X's pontificate "most people deemed him very chaste; however, he was afterward discovered to be exceedingly devoted, and every day with less and less shame, to that kind of pleasure that for honor's sake may not be named."

Sixtus IV was one of several popes suspected of being homosexual. The basis of this being the diary of Stefano Infessura (1440–1500) who recorded documented episodes and unsubstantiated rumors. This included accusations of Sixtus awarding benefices and bishoprics in return for sexual favors.... However, an exception was was Giovanni Sclafenato, who was made a cardinal, according to the papal epitaph on his tomb, for 'ingenuousness, loyalty and his others gifts of soul and body.' "

Pope Paul III was said to have "murdered relatives, including poisoning his mother and niece, to inherit the family fortune.... The most famous anecdote about Paul III's ruthlessness revolved around a theological dispute between two cardinals and a Polish bishop." When the argument became tedious, Paul III had all three hacked to death with swords.

Once a man is elected Pope he can only be validly removed from office by resignation or death. There is no impeachment procedure for Popes.

Vatican archives testify that in the centuries after Leo the Great saved Rome from Attila's sacking Huns, Lucius III instigated the Inquisition; Pope Innocent III "exercised effective political control over all Italy and much of Europe to bring the temporal power of the Papacy to its highwater mark; Leo X...excommunicated Martin Luther and proved incapable of dealing with the Reformation; Alexander VI (a Borgia) practiced simony and nepotism and failed in his master plan to conquer and unify Italy; Pius VII signed a Concordat with Napoleon and restored Catholicism to France; Leo XIII issued an encyclical, *Rerum Novarum*, that first diagnosed for Roman Catholics the sickness of contemporary society and called on them to cure it—unsuccessfully."

As one historian notes, the Roman Catholic Church is humanity's oldest continuing institution, spanning two millennia. For centuries, the church has been happy to operate away from the public eye, but a written record of the Church and most of its papal history can be found in the Vatican's immense archives, including Clement V's dissolution of the Knights Templar and the assertion by the director of the Vatican's observatory that if there are intelligent beings beyond the bounds of Earth, they are, like us, the handiwork of God.

Among the dark secrets that some people believe may be held by the Vatican's present ruler are those that set the date for the end of the world as we know it, the fulfillment of the prophesies of the book of Revelations, and the return of Christ.

CHAPTER 14

Myths, Rumors, and Presidents

The late Jesuit priest, scholar, Vatican insider, and best-selling author Malachi Martin said, "Anybody who is acquainted with the state of affairs in the Vatican is well aware that the prince of darkness has had and still has his surrogates in the court of St. Peter in Rome."

From 1958 until 1964, Martin served in Rome where he was a close associate of, and carried out many sensitive missions for Pope Paul VI. Released frm his vows of poverty and obedience at his own request (but still a priest), he ultimately moved to New York and became a best-selling writer of fiction and nonfiction. In his first reference to a diabolic rite held in Rome in his 1990 nonfiction best-seller about geopolitics and the Vatican, *The Keys of This Blood*, he wrote, "Pope Paul had come up against the irremovable presence of a malign strength in his own Vatican and in certain bishops' chanceries. It was what knowledgeable Churchmen called the 'superforce.' Rumors, always difficult to verify, tied its installation to the beginning of Pope Paul VI's reign in 1963."

Indeed, Pope Paul VI had alluded somberly to "the smoke of Satan which has entered the Sanctuary."

In 1996 in *Windswept House: A Vatican Novel*, Martin vividly described a ceremony called "The Enthronement of the Fallen Archangel Lucifer" supposedly held in St. Paul's Chapel in the Vatican on June 29, 1963, barely a week after the election of Paul VI. In the novel, before he dies, a Pope leaves a secret account of the situation on his desk for the next occupant of the throne of Peter, a thinly disguised reference to John Paul II.

According to *The New American* magazine, Martin confirmed the ceremony did indeed occur as he had described. "Oh yes, it is true; very much so," he said. "But the only way I could put that down into print is in novelistic form."

A symbol of Satan was said to be a bent crucifix with a repulsive or distorted figure representing Christ. Historians note that it was a sinister symbol used by sixth century Satanists and black magicians and sorcerers in the Middle Ages to represent the "mark of the beast." During the reigns of both Popes Paul VI and John Paul II, a papal staff with the Twisted Cross was continually held before adoring masses of Catholic faithful, who were unaware that they were adoring a symbol that was once the sign of the Antichrist. This crucifix is also carried by Benedict XVI.

"There is a greater openness towards the devil,' said Father Gabriele Amorth, the Vatican's Chief Exorcist, to the Christian Broadcasting Network in 2008.

Father Pedro Barrajon, a priest in Rome, stated, "Satanism and the occult are in fashion. The overwhelmingly Roman Catholic nation of Italy has an estimated 800 satanic cults, with more than 600,000 followers. But Rome, home to Vatican City and the pope, is where the fiercest spiritual battle is taking place."

A persistent and false belief is that the Vatican Library contains the world's largest collection of pornography, that the Vatican holds many secret documents the Catholic Church doesn't want the world to see, and that the archives hold thousands of papers that would question the power and authority of the Church.

It is sometimes claimed by non-scholars that some of these directly refer to Jesus, such as the execution order for Jesus signed by Pontius Pilate, or items that were personally written by Jesus, explaining to his followers how to conduct the formation of the Catholic Church after his death, or even the exact date of his return to judge mankind. There has been only one document attributed to Jesus himself. It is known as the Letter of Christ and Abgarus. Scholars generally believe that it was fabricated, probably in the third century AD. There is no evidence that Jesus wrote anything during his life, except unknown words inscribed in dust on the ground when he was questioned about a woman caught in adultery.

The Catholic Church does have all records that passed through the Vatican in the Library at the Vatican, including every letter written by the Popes. Some contain questionable decisions made by past popes. The Archives also contain letters to the popes, including communications from England on the subject of King Henry VIII's demands for papal approval of the dissolution of his marriage to Queen Catherine of Aragon so Henry could wed Anne Boleyn.

A misconception surrounding the Papal Tiara suggests that the words Vicarius Filii Dei (Latin for "Vicar of the Son of God") exist on the side of one of the tiaras.

This story centers on a widely made claim that when the letters are given numbers based on alphabetical sequence and are added, they total 666, described in the Book of Revelation as the number of the Beast (the Antichrist) who wears multiple crowns. This claim has been made by some Protestant sects who believe that the Pope, as the head of the Roman Catholic Church is the Beast or the False Prophet. The Vatican notes that a detailed examination of the tiaras shows no such decoration, and that Vicarius Filii Dei is not among the titles of the Pope. The Vatican states that the closest match is Vicarius Christi ("Vicar of Christ"), which does not add up to 666.

A popular myth holds that there was once a Pope Joan. A claim that a woman held the papacy first appeared in a Dominican chronicle in 1250. It soon spread in Europe through traveling friars. The time period for this claim is traditionally given as AD 855–858, between the reigns of Leo IV and Benedict III, but this is impossible because Leo IV died on July 17, 855, and Pope Benedict III was elected two months later (September 29). Jean de Mailly, a French Dominican at Metz, placed the story in 1099 in his *Chronica universalis mettensis*, which dates from around 1250, and gave what is almost certainly the earliest authentic account of a woman who became known as Pope Joan.

In Vatican lore there are two versions of the Pope Joan legend. In the first, an English woman, called Joan, went to Athens with her lover to study there. In the second, a German woman called Giliberta was born in Mainz. This "Joan" disguised herself as a monk, called Joannes Anglicus. In time, she rose to the highest office of the Church. After two or five years of reign, Pope Joan became pregnant, and during an Easter procession, she gave birth on the streets when she fell off a horse. She was publicly stoned to death by the astonished crowd. According to the legend, she was removed from the Vatican archives. As a consequence, popes in the medieval period were required to undergo a procedure wherein they sat on a special chair with a hole in the seat. A cardinal would have the task of putting his hand up the hole to check whether the pope had testicles. In a seventeenth-century study, Protestant historian David Blondel argued that "Pope Joan" was a fictitious story that may have been a satire that came to be believed as reality.

While the popularity of the legend is mysterious, to Vatican historians there is no doubt it is legend. There are no contemporary references to a woman pope, and there is no room in the acknowledged papal chronology to fit her in

During the reign of Paul VI, rumors flew in Rome and throughout Italy that he was homosexual. It was whispered that when he was the Archbishop of Milan, he was caught by police one night wearing civilian clothes and with what was called "not so laudable company." Vatican insiders claimed that for many years he had a special friendship with a red-haired actor. This man made no secret of his relationship with the future pope. The relationship allegedly continued and became even closer. After Cardinal Montini became Pope Paul VI, an official of the Vatican security forces alleged that "this favorite of Montini" was allowed to come and go freely in the pontifical apartments, and that he was seen taking the papal elevator at night.

Although the United States has been a predominately Protestant nation, the papacy has drawn the attention of every president in the last half of the twentieth century. The first papal audience with a president occurred shortly after the end of the First World War, when Woodrow Wilson was received at the Vatican by Pope Benedict XV in 1919. The next wasn't for forty more years, when President Dwight Eisenhower saw Pope John XXIII in Rome.

President Kennedy had an audience with Pope Paul VI on July 3, 1963, within days of Paul VI's coronation. Since then, every president has met with the pope at least once, often more. President Lyndon Johnson was host to Paul VI during a papal visit to the United States. Jimmy Carter hailed John Paul II as the pontiff toured six American cities in the fall of 1979 as a "messenger of brotherhood and peace." On October 6, Carter became the first president to welcome a pope to the White House.

In the 1980s, Ronald Reagan and John Paul II became allies against the Soviet Union and are credited with winning the Cold War. Reagan began formal diplomatic relations in 1984. Before the establishment of the official contacts, Myron Taylor served during World War II as emissary for President Roosevelt. President Harry Truman's pick of a WWII hero Mark W. Clark was defeated by the Senate. Between 1951 and 1968, the United States had no official representative accredited to the Holy See. President Nixon changed this when he appointed Henry Cabot Lodge, Jr. as his personal representative. President Carter followed with the appointment of former New York City mayor Robert F. Wagner, Jr. Every ambassador to date has been a Roman Catholic.

The close contact between Reagan and John Paul II continued under George H.W. Bush and Bill Clinton. But George W. Bush became the record-holder in papal visits, with a total of five meetings with two popes, John Paul II and his successor. In June 2008 when he visited Pope Benedict XVI, they spoke in a garden where the pontiff prayed daily, rather than in the library where Benedict greeted most world leaders. This sparked rumors that President Bush might convert to Catholicism. Vatican observers described him as the most "Catholic-minded" president since John F. Kennedy "The rosy legend of a possible conversion of Bush to Catholicism has started to circulate," wrote Marco Politi, Vatican correspondent of *La Repubblica*, after the chat in the papal garden. Politi noted that the president's brother Jeb had converted to Roman Catholicism, as had former British Prime Minister Tony Blair.

The White House called reports of President Bush converting to

Catholicism "baseless speculation." Father Richard John Neuhaus, a prominent Catholic priest who ran the monthly magazine *First Things* said, "I'd be very surprised."

When the Vatican wants to let the world know something, it is most likely to make the announcement in the newspaper *L'Osservatore Romano*. Founded in 1861, it has served as a mouthpiece of Vatican news, reporting the daily routines of popes and providing ample space for their writings, often in Latin. It was also considered a clearing house for semiofficial thinking on touchy issues such as birth control and women in the clergy.

An article in the *Wall Street Journal* in October 2008 noted that the paper has long drawn criticism, "often from within the highest ranks of the church." In 1961, Cardinal Giovanni Battista Montini, then the Archbishop of Milan, penned a stinging critique of the publication on its 100th anniversary. "Even when the headline page is not in Latin, one cannot always say that it provides enjoyable reading," wrote the future Pope Paul VI. "A serious newspaper, a grave newspaper, but who would ever read it on the tram or at the bar, who would ever strike up a discussion about it?"

The decades that followed were ones of steady decline. It currently has a circulation of about 15,000.

In May 2008, L'Osservatore Romano ran an interview with the Vatican's top astronomer. "If we consider earthly creatures as 'brother' and 'sister,' why cannot we also speak of an 'extraterrestrial brother?'" mused Father José Gabriel Funes, director of the Vatican Observatory. Pressed on whether Heaven might be open to such alien beings, the Rev. Funes said, "Jesus has been incarnated once, for everyone."

Perhaps more surprising than a Vatican star-gazer's openness to the idea of life elsewhere in the universe is that some people believe the darkest Vatican secret is that it has proof such creatures have paid visits to Earth.

CHAPTER 15

And God Created Aliens

E nergized by the statement by the head of the Vatican's observatory that there was no conflict between the tenets of the Church and belief in extraterrestrial life, adherents of the theory that unidentified objects in the sky (UFOs) carry beings from outer space contend that the Vatican has known about them since the 1950s. It is said by UFO exponents, who communicate with each other primarily via the Internet, that Pope Pius XII decided to create a secret information department with a structure similar to the military intelligence departments of the United States and Britain. Its purpose was to gather all possible information regarding the activities of the alien entities and information acquired by the U.S. Air Force in its investigations of UFO reports. The codename for this program was said to be "Secretum Omega."

One Internet site asserted that skeletal remains resembling space aliens had been excavated from the basement floor of a centuries old vault under the Vatican Library. According to this report, the discovery occurred because the library was undergoing a major restoration to its underground vaults, containing dirt floors that had not felt a human foot in more than 500 years.

Another website presented an enlarged, technically enhanced photograph of a purported UFO hovering near the dome of St. Peter's Basilica, taken by a Polish tourist in St. Peter's Square on June 24, 2006.

Numerous contributors to UFO chat rooms find evidence of life beyond Earth in the Bible. They interpret the Prophet Ezekhial seeing "a wheel, way up in the middle of the air; the big wheel ran by faith and the little wheel ran by the grace of God, a wheel in a wheel, away in the middle of the air." These wheels were turning, one wheel within the other. Also cited was Jacob in the book of Genesis seeing a ladder set up on the earth that reached to heaven; and "behold, the angels of God were ascending and descending."

UFO believers cited news coverage of Pope John Paul II lying in state that purportedly showed an unidentified flying object over St. Peter's Basilica.

Should it prove to be true that the Vatican has secret files on UFOs and beings from outer space, it's nothing new. In the fifteenth century, Cardinal Nicolo Cusano (1401–1464), philosopher and scientist, said, "We are not authorized to exclude that on another star beings do exist, even if they are completely different from us."

While Vatican astronomers search the skies in the hope of learning about the secrets of the universe, archeologists have been exploring beneath the Vatican to learn more about the origins of the Church. Excavations began in June 1939. They found that two levels below St. Peter's Basilica lies an excavated Roman graveyard full of mausoleums, frescoes, inscriptions and stucco decorations. It was here in the 1940s that experts uncovered the bones of a tall man whose grave had been venerated in early times. Many thought they were the bones of St. Peter, believed to have been martyred in Nero's Circus nearby. But *Time* magazine noted, "What the excavators found was a looted grave, so despoiled (probably by the Saracens in 846) that much of it was a featureless hole. There was no trace of the bronze casket in which tradition said Constantine had placed St. Peter's relics. All that remained, buried at the rear of the grave niche, were a few bones. The Vatican has said only that they are human, that there is no skull among them, and that they are those of a powerfully built person of advanced age but undetermined sex."

In June 1968, Pope Paul VI announced that bones unearthed during the excavations under St. Peter's Basilica were, in his judgment, those of Peter the Apostle. "The relics of St. Peter," he declared, "have been identified in a manner which we believe convincing."

He based his conclusion on "very patient and accurate investigations" by "worthy and competent persons."

Vatican archeologists also believed that they identified the tomb of St. Paul in the Roman basilica that bears his name. A sarcophagus was identified in the basilica of St. Paul. The sarcophagus was discovered during excavations carried out in 2002 and 2003 around the basilica, in the south of Rome."The tomb that we discovered," said archaeologist Giorgio Filippi," is the one that the popes and the Emperor Theodosius (379–395) saved and presented to the whole world as being the tomb of the apostle."

The discovery was made by a team composed exclusively of experts from the Vatican Museum. They had undertaken their exploration in response to a request from the administrator of St. Paul's basilica, Archbishop Francesco Gioia. During the Jubilee Year 2000, the archbishop noticed that thousands of pilgrims were inquiring about the location of St. Paul's tomb. The excavation effort was guided by nineteenth century plans for the basilica, which was largely rebuilt after a fire in 1823. An initial survey enabled archeologists to reconstruct the shape of the original basilica, built early in the fourth century. A second excavation, under the main altar of the basilica, brought the Vatican team to the sarcophagus, which was located on what would have been ground level for the original fourth-century building.

The Catholic World News Service reported that under the altar a marble plaque was still visible. Dating back to the fourth century, it bore the inscription: "Apostle Paul, martyr."

As an archeologist, Filippi said that he had no special curiosity to learn whether the remains of St. Paul were still inside that sarcophagus. He said that the tomb should not be opened merely to satisfy curiosity, but he had no doubt that St. Paul was buried on the site, "because this basilica was the object of pilgrimages by emperors; people from all around the world came to venerate him, having faith that he was present in this basilica."

In 2007, Pope Benedict XVI gave his approval to plans by investigators to examine the interior of the ancient stone coffin. They were given permission to remove a plug with which the coffin had been sealed so an endoscopic probe could be inserted and the contents viewed.

While excavations were being carried out inside Vatican City in 2003 for an underground garage to ease the Vatican's parking problems a 2,000-year-old burial ground was discovered. The necropolis, which traces pagan Rome to the birth of Christianity, contained more than forty elaborately decorated mausoleums and 200 individual tombs. Headstones, including one that belonged to a slave of Nero, urns and elaborately decorated frescoes and mosaic floors were uncovered on the site.

The historical importance of the find was described as second only to the necropolis below St Peter's Basilica. The *Guardian* of London reported that Giandomenico Spinola, director of the project, described the necropolis as being in an excellent condition because it had been protected by a landslide at the end of the second century. Most of the tombs dated between the era of Augustus (23B.C.–A.D.14) to that of Constantine (306–337).

A monument to Pope Leo XI, a Medici, in white marble, by Alessandro Algardi (1645–1646), took much longer to create than Leo XI reigned. Seventy years old and rather frail when he was elected, he was the 232nd pope and died just twenty-six days into his reign (April 1–27, 1605). Born in Florence, he was the last of the Medici family's popes. His mother, Francesca Salviati, was a daughter of Giacomo Salviati and Lucrezia de' Medici, a sister of Leo X, while his father, Ottaviano, was a more distant scion of the Medici family. King Henry IV of France, who had learned to like Leo XI when he was papal legate at his court, is said to have bankrolled promotion of his election. When Leo took sick after his coronation, he was importuned by many members of the Curia to make one of his grandnephews a cardinal, but Leo had such an aversion to nepotism that he refused. When his confessor urged him to grant it, he dismissed him and sent for another. Because of the brevity of his papacy, the Italians called him Papa Lampo (Lightning Pope).

Algardi also memorialized Pope Leo I, who saved Rome from Attila when the Mongolian conqueror, King of the Huns, was ready and waiting to cross the Po River with his horde and attack the city. Leo, in papal robes, entered Attila's camp, stood before Attila, and threatened him with the power from St. Peter if he did not turn back and leave Italy unmolested. When Attila agreed to turn back, his servants reportedly asked him why he had capitulated so easily to the Bishop of Rome. Attila answered that all the while the Pope was speaking, there had appeared in the sky above the Pope's head a vision of St. Peter with drawn sword.

A papal tomb not found in the Vatican is that of Pope Alexander VI.

Historian Elizabeth Lev wrote that generally in the history of the papacy, Pope Alexander VI does not make it into the list of the top ten, twenty or thirty. She wrote, "Alexander became to the papacy what Nero is to the Roman empire, the Pope critics love to hate." Born Roderigo Borgia in 1431 near Valencia, Spain, he rose to the rank of cardinal with the help of his uncle Pope Callistus III, then, as a favorite of Isabella and Ferdinand of Spain, he was elected Pope in 1492 while Columbus was discovering America in the employ of the same Spanish sovereigns. Contemporaries viewed this election with much trepidation, Lev noted, because all the contracts and titles related to the vast enterprise of the New World would be in Spanish hands.

Alexander did little to court public opinion, exasperating many by leading an openly licentious life and favoring his children, particularly Cesare Borgia, who was accused of several murders during Alexander's pontificate and was protected if not abetted by his father. Alexander VI fathered seven children, including Lucrezia and Cesare Borgia, by at least two mistresses. Such was Alexander VI's unpopularity that when he died, perhaps by poisoning, perhaps from the plague, in 1503 at the age of seventy-two, the priests of St Peter's Basilica at first refused to accept his body for burial. He died on August 18, 1503, in the twelfth year of his pontificate. He was buried on August 19 in the church of Santa Maria della Febbre, Rome, and his body was transferred in 1610 to the church of Santa Maria di Monserrato in Rome.

More than four centuries after the dome of St. Peter's basilica was completed, the Vatican announced the discovery of a long-missing Michelangelo sketch for the dome, possibly his last design before his death. Drawn in blood-red chalk for the stone cutters who were working on the basilica, it was done in the spring of 1563, less than a year before his death at age ninety. The sketch was found in the Fabbrica of St. Peter's, which contains the basilica's offices.

The newspaper *L'Osservatore Romano* said most sketches by Michelangelo for the stone cutters were destroyed or lost in the cutters' workplaces, but this one had survived because a supervisor used the back of the sketch to make notes of problems linked to the stone's transport through the outskirts of Rome. Michelangelo finished the dome and four columns for its base before he died in February 1564. Three weeks before he died, when he was nearly eighty-nine, he went up the dome to inspect it.

The construction of the basilica, whose cupola defines Rome's skyline, spanned several working lifetimes of some of the Renaissance's most celebrated artists and architects. Vatican historians note that the first architect of the basilica, Donato Bramante, died eight years after the cornerstone was laid. Other architects, including Raphael, followed, until Pope Paul III turned to Michelangelo in 1546, thirty-two years after Michelangelo had put his last brush stroke on the frescoes of the Sistine Chapel's ceiling.

Also in 2007, the Associated Press reported that a 450-year-old receipt found in the same archive provided proof that Michelangelo had kept a private room in St. Peter's Basilica while working as the pope's chief architect. Going through archives for an exhibit on the 500th anniversary of the basilica, researchers from the Fabbrica di San Pietro came across an entry for a key to a chest located "in the room in St. Peter's where Master Michelangelo retires."

"We now know that Michelangelo definitely had a private space in the basilica," said Maria Cristina Carlo-Stella, who runs the Fabbrica, in an interview with the Associated Press. "The next step is to identify it."

The ink-scripted entry contained in a parchment-covered volume listing the expenditures of the Fabbrica for the years 1556–58, referred to the payment of ten scudos to the blacksmith who forged the key, but offered no details about the chest or the location of the room.

The account of the discovery noted that a frescoed room with a cozy fireplace, part of the area in the left wing of the basilica where the archives are housed, had traditionally been called "la stanza di Michelangelo" (Michelangelo's room). On an upper floor, overlooking the main altar, it is connected to the ground floor by a small winding marble staircase, suggesting that the room afforded the artist secrecy and an escape route from envious fellow artisans. But research showed the room was part of renovation done after Michelangelo's death, and that the space did not exist during Michelangelo's time at the Vatican.

""The theory is very romantic and conspiratorial, but totally unfounded," said Federico Bellini, an art historian who worked in the archive department.

Originally the Fabbrica, whose documents date from as far back as 1506, was in the right wing of the basilica, already built at the time of Michelangelo. It was known that artisans had been allotted lodgings there, leading experts to direct their search for Michelangelo's studio to that area.

The Associated Press article noted, "One detail the expenditure does reveal is that Michelangelo had requested a very expensive key. According to Simona Turriziani, a Fabbrica archivist, ten scudos in the 1550s was more than the monthly salary of many of the artisans working on the basilica."

CHAPTER 16

The Vatican and the
End of the World

In the spring of 1916 in the town of Fatima, Portugal, three shepherd girls, Lucia dos Santos and her cousins Jacinta and Francisca Marto, were visited three times by what they thought was an angel. He "told them he was the guardian angel of Portugal and urged them to pray and prepare themselves. The next spring, eight months after the angel's final visit, the Virgin Mary began to speak to them. Lucia had just had her tenth birthday, Francisco would turn nine in June, and Jacinta was seven. On May 13, 1917, they took their sheep to a small hollow known as a *Cova da Iria* (Cove of Irene). And there around noon, a beautiful lady appeared near an oak tree, telling them to say the Rosary every day, 'to bring peace to the world and an end to the war.' She promised to visit them again 'on the thirteenth of each month' for the next five months.'

"By 1917, a figure who identified herself as the Virgin appeared to them and eventually delivered a message for humankind. The children became a focus of worldwide interest, and in October of that year, the Virgin's presence seemed to be confirmed for many others when a crowd of 70,000—mostly Catholics and some skeptics—saw the sun appear to zigzag in the sky as the Virgin again addressed the children.

"I looked at the sun and saw it spinning like a disc, rolling on itself," said a farmer, Antonio de Oliveiro. "I saw people changing color. They were stained with the colors of the rainbow. The sun seemed to fall down from the sky. The people said that the world was going to end. They were afraid and screaming."

Maria Candida da Silva said, "Suddenly the rain stopped and a great splendor appeared and the children cried, 'Look at the sun!' I saw the sun coming down, feeling that it was falling to the ground. At that moment, I collapsed."

The Reverend Joao Menitra reported, "I looked and saw that the people were in various colors, yellow, white, blue. At the same time, I beheld the sun spinning at great speed and very near me. I at once thought: I am going to die."

"Fatima almost immediately became a global pilgrimage site.

"The message delivered there remained a mystery as the children refused to reveal the content of the vision. Two of them died in childhood during an epidemic; but in 1941, Lucia, the survivor by then a nun, released a description of the first two 'secrets' from the Virgin that made headlines all over the world. One was a vivid vision of Hell; the other was a prediction that World War I would end, but if people continued to offend God, a worse one would break out during the Pontificate of Pius XI."

Regarding the first secret's vision of Hell, Lucia said, "Our Lady showed us a great sea of fire which seemed to be under the earth. Plunged in this fire were demons and souls in human form, like transparent burning embers, all blackened or burnished bronze, floating about in the conflagration, now raised into the air by the flames that issued from within themselves together with great clouds of smoke, now falling back on every side like sparks in a huge fire, without weight or equilibrium, and amid shrieks and groans of pain and despair, which horrified us and made us tremble with fear. The demons could be distinguished by their terrifying and repulsive likeness to frightful and unknown animals, all black and transparent."

This vision lasted but an instant, Lucia said, "Otherwise, I think we would have died of fear and terror."

"The second secret was a statement that World War I would end and supposedly predicted the coming of World War II, should God continue to be offended and if Russia did not convert. The second half requested that Russia be consecrated to the Immaculate Heart.

In 1941, a document was written by Lucia at the request of Jose da Silva, Bishop of Leiria, to assist with the publication of a new edition of a book on Jacinta. "When asked by the Bishop of Leiria in 1943 to reveal the secret, Lucia struggled for a short period, being 'not yet convinced that God had clearly authorized her to act. However, in October of 1943 the bishop of Leiria ordered her to put it in writing. Lucia then wrote the secret down and sealed it in an envelope not to be opened until 1960, when 'it will appear clearer.'…

"In June of 1944, the sealed envelope containing the third secret was delivered to Silva, where it stayed until 1957, when it was finally delivered to Rome."

"To ensure better protection for the 'secret.' the envelope was placed in the Secret Archives of the Holy Office on April 4, 1957.

"According to the records of the Archives, the Commissary of the Holy Office, Father Pierre Paul Philippe, with the agreement of Cardinal Alfredo Ottaviani, brought the envelope containing the third part of the 'secret of Fatima' to Pope John XXIII on August 17, 1959. After some hesitation, His Holiness said, 'We shall wait. I shall pray. I shall let you know what I decide.'

"In fact, Pope John XXIII decided to return the sealed envelope to the Holy Office and not to reveal the third part of the 'secret.'

"Pope Paul VI read the contents…on March 27, 1965, and returned the envelope to the Archives of the Holy Office, deciding not to publish the text.

"John Paul II…asked for the envelope containing the third part of the secret following the assassination attempt on May 13, 1981. On July 18, 1981 Cardinal Franjo Šeper, Prefect of the Congregation, gave two envelopes to Archbishop Eduardo Martínez Somalo, Substitute of the Secretariat of State: one was a white envelope, containing Sister Lucia's original text in Portuguese; the other orange, with the Italian translation of the 'secret.' [On] August 11, Archbishop Martínez returned the two envelopes to the Archives of the Holy Office."

"The text of the third secret was officially released by Pope John Paul II in 2000." He claimed that the third secret was a prediction of the attempt on his life, and that he had been saved because the Virgin Mary deflected the bullet.

Doubters claimed that it was not the real secret revealed by Lucia, "despite assertions from the Vatican to the contrary."

Along with the text of the secret, the future Pope, Cardinal Joseph Ratzinger, published a theological commentary, in which he stated that a careful reading of the text of the so-called third secret of Fatima would "probably prove disappointing or surprising after all the speculation it has stirred."

No great mystery was revealed, he said, "nor is the future unveiled."

After explaining the differences between public and private revelations, he cautioned people not to see in the message a determined future event. He said, "The purpose of the vision is not to show a film of an irrevocably fixed future. Its meaning is exactly the opposite: it is meant to mobilize the forces of change in the right direction. Therefore we must totally discount fatalistic explanations of the 'secret,' such as, for example, the claim that the would-be assassin of 13 May 1981 was merely an instrument of the divine plan guided by Providence and could not therefore have acted freely, or other similar ideas in circulation. Rather, the vision speaks of dangers and how we might be saved from them."

According to the *New York Times*, speculation over the content of the secret ranged "from worldwide nuclear annihilation to deep rifts in the Roman Catholic Church that lead to rival papacies.

"There were some groups who disputed that the full text of the third secret had been officially published. The most prominent among these was The Fatima Center, which is run by Father Nicholas Gruner, who was suspended as a priest by the Avellino, Italy, diocese. Father Gruner rejected the validity of the suspension and continued to perform the functions of a priest. On November 22, 2006, the Italian author Antonio Socci published *Il Quarto Segreto di Fatima* (*The Fourth Secret of Fatima*) in Italian, which also argued that the Vatican had not formally released the entire Third Secret. These critics...pointed to the fact that Lucia's vision, as recorded in the officially released text, did not contain any words from Mary, as one might expect, and it said nothing about a crisis of faith in the Church.

"The Vatican maintained its position that the full text of the Third Secret was published in June 2000." Although the Holy See claimed that publication of the third [and last] of secrets given by the Virgin Mary to three children at Fatima, Portugal, in 1917 predicted the 1981 attempted assassination of John Paul II, it was believed by many Catholics and others that the final forecast also gave the date for the Second Coming of Christ, and the end of the world as we know it.

While the New Testament's book of Revelations by St. John of Patmos is the Christian foretelling of the climax of history and the Second Coming of Christ, the Vatican Archives contain other doomsday prophecies. Johannes Friede (1204–57) provided a glimpse of global warming. He wrote, "When the great time will come, in which mankind will face its last, hard trial, it will be foreshadowed by striking changes in nature. The alteration between cold and heat will become more intensive, storms will have more catastrophic effects, earthquakes will destroy great regions, and the seas will overflow many lowlands. Not all of it will be the result of natural causes, but mankind will penetrate into the bowels of the earth and will reach into the clouds, gambling with its own existence. Before the powers of destruction will succeed in their design, the universe will be thrown into disorder, and the age of iron will plunge into nothingness. When nights will be filled with more intensive cold and days with heat, a new life will begin in nature. The heat means radiation from the earth, the cold the waning light of the sun. Only a few years more and you will become aware that sunlight has grown perceptibly weaker. When even your artificial light will cease to give service, the great event in the heavens will be near."

In the sixteenth century, Maria Laach Monastery looked ahead four hundred years and said, "The twentieth century will bring death and destruction, apostasy from the Church, discord in families, cities and governments; it will be the century of three great wars with intervals of a few decades. They will become ever more devastating and bloody and will lay in ruins not only Germany, but finally all countries of East and West. After a terrible defeat of Germany will follow the next great war. There will be no bread for people anymore and no fodder for animals. Poisonous clouds, manufactured by human hands, will sink down and exterminate everything. The human mind will be seized by insanity."

Perhaps the most famous and controversial predictions were made in the eleventh century by an Irishman. Canonized by Pope Clement III in 1190, the first papal canonization of an Irish saint, he was born in Armagh in 1094, ostensibly of noble birth. He was baptized Máel Máedóc (a name that has been Latinized as Malachy) and ordained at age twenty-five. In 1123, his uncle, "the lay abbot of Bangor, resigned in favor of Malachy. In 1125, he was chosen Bishop of Connor and Down...and set to work teaching and proclaiming the Gospel," established a seminary, and restored churches. In 1129, he became Archbishop of Armagh.

"In 1137, Malachy set out for Rome. On the way, he stayed at Clairvaux and became friends with St. Bernard. When he arrived in Rome, Malachy tried to resign and become a monk at Clairvaux, but Pope Innocent II refused and instead appointed him Papal Legate to Ireland."

"While on his way to the Vatican in 1139 to assume the post of papal legate for Ireland, he fell into trance and saw a line of papal reigns stretching from the successor to Innocent II and extending through centuries to the last of the line.... Malachy assigned short descriptions in Latin to each pope, referring to a family name, birthplace, coat-of-arms, or office held before election to the papacy.... He wrote poetic descriptions of each of the pontiffs, and presented the manuscript to Pope Innocent II—and it was forgotten until 1590. It has been in print—and hotly debated for both authenticity and correctness, ever since."

Malachy's Prohecies: The Last Ten Popes

"The Burning Fire": Pius X (1903–14) It has been said that this Pope showed a burning passion for the spiritual renewal of the Church.

"Religion Laid Waste": Benedict XV (1914–22) "During this Pope's reign, [the world] saw Communism move into Russia where religious life was laid waste, and World War I, with the death of millions of Christians."

"Unshaken Faith": Pius XI (1922–39) "This Pope faced tremendous pressure from fascist and sinister powers in Germany and Italy, but he was an outspoken critic of Communism and Fascism which enraged Hitler."

"An Angelic Shepherd": Pius XII (1939–58) This Pope had an affinity for the spiritual world and was a beloved and admired pontiff throughout World War II.

"Pastor and Mariner": John XXIII (1958–63) John was a pastor to the world, much beloved, and the Patriarch of Venice. The connection to 'mariner' is thus remarkable."

"Flower of Flowers": Paul VI (1963–78) "Paul's coat-of-arms depicted three fleurs-de-lis (iris blossoms), corresponding to Malachy's prophecy."

"Of the Half Moon": John Paul I (1978–78) "Elected Pope on August 26, 1978, when there was a half moon…who was born in the diocese of Belluno (beautiful moon) and was baptized Albino Luciani (white light). He became pope on August 26, 1978, when the moon appeared exactly half full in its waning phase. He died in the following month, soon after an eclipse of the moon."

"The Labor of the Sun": John Paul II (1978–2005) "Pope John Paul II was the most traveled Pope in history. He circled the globe numerous times, preaching to huge audiences everywhere he went.…He was born on May 18, 1920. On that date in the morning there was a near total eclipse of the sun over Europe. Prophecy—the 110th Pope is 'De Labore Solis' (Of the Solar Eclipse, or, From the Toil of the Sun). Like the sun he came out of the East (Poland)."

"The Glory of the Olive": Benedict XVI (2005–   ) "The Order of St. Benedict has said this Pope will come from their order. Jesus gave his apocalyptic prophecy about the end of time from the Mount of Olives. This

Pope will reign during the beginning of the tribulation of which Jesus spoke. The 111th prophesy is 'Gloria Olivae' (The Glory of the Olive)....
Saint Benedict himself prophesied that before the end of the world his Order, known also as the Olivetans, would triumphantly lead the Roman Catholic Church in its fight against evil.

"Peter the Roman." "This final Pope will be Satan, taking the form of a man named Peter who will gain a worldwide allegiance and adoration. He will be the final antichrist of which prophecy students have long fore-told."

According to Malachy's prophecies, there will be only one Pope after the reign of Benedict XVI. But the prevailing view of the Vatican today is that they are elaborate forgeries, possibly the work of Jesuit monks in the 1600s. The Catholic Encyclopedia noted, "The last of these prophecies concerns the end of the world and is as follows: 'In the final persecution of the Holy Roman Church there will reign Peter the Roman, who will feed his flock amid many tribulations, after which the seven-hilled city will be destroyed and the dreadful Judge will judge the people.'"

It has been noticed concerning Petrus Romanus that the prophecy does not say no popes will intervene between him and his predecessor desig-nated Gloria olivae [Benedict XVI]. It merely says that he is to be the last pope, leaving the possibility of other popes before "Peter the Roman."

Those who cast doubt on St. Malachy's forecast of the last in the long line of the papacy as a prophecy of the end of the world hasten to point out that Jesus Christ declared in the Gospel of Matthew, 26:36, "No one knows about that day or hour, not even the angels in heaven, nor the Son, but only the Father."

Vatican Library Chronology

This chronology is from New Advent, "The Vatican and Its History" at www.ibiblio.org/expo/vatican.exhibit/exhibit/History.html.

1451   Pope Nicholas V conceives of a library "for the common convenience of the learned," and the Vatican Library is born. Nicholas's collection numbered about 1,160 books.

1475   Pope Sixtus IV brings the Library to life, installing the books in a restored suite of rooms, building up the collection, and naming Bartolomeo Platina as the Vatican's first formal librarian.

1470   During the High Renaissance, the Library grew enormously. By
−1525   1481, a handwritten catalog by Platina shows 3,500 entries. As from its inception, the collections are available without restriction regarding the reader's religious or other views.

1517   Protestant Reformation begins.

1570   Counter-Reformation. The Library inevitably suffers from the
−1610   introduction of the Index of banned books (1558) and some limitations on access are imposed.

1623   Most of the rich holdings of the Palatine Library in the Protestant stronghold of Heidelberg become part of the Vatican Library collection as war booty.

MID−1600s   The Library again welcomes unfettered scholarly pursuit, including by Protestants. It acquires vast new holdings of manuscripts and books, most notably a spectacular assortment of items from distant lands.

1785   Pope Pius VI strictly limits the consultation of manuscripts, prompting Spanish priest Juan Andres to accuse the pope of overseeing a "cemetery of books not a library."

1883   Pope Leo XIII formally declares the Library open to qualified
            researchers.

1927–39   The Library of Congress and the Carnegie Endowment for Inter-
            national Peace help modernize the Vatican Library's book catalog
            system.

1992   Vatican Library holdings number almost 2 million printed books and
            serials; 75,000 Latin, Greek, Arabic, Hebrew, Persian, Ethiopian,
            Syriac and other manuscripts from the 2nd Century A.D. on; 65,000
            units of archival volumes in 23 deposits or fondi; 100,000 prints,
            engravings, maps and drawings; 330,000 Greek, Roman and papal
            coins and medals.

2007   Publication of the Chinon Parchment of 1308 exonerating the
            Knights Templar of charges of heresy.

2007–10   Closes to the public for renovations/rebuilding for first time in 500
            years.

Vatican Archives Chronology

This chronology is from Wikipedia, "Vatican Secret Archives" at en.wikipedia.org/wiki/Vatican_Secret_Archives.

1883   Pope Leo XIII opened archives dated 1815 or earlier to nonclerical scholars.

1924   Documents opened to the end of the pontificate of Gregory XVI (1846).

1966   Documents opened from the pontificate of Pius IX (1846–78).

1978   Documents opened from the pontificate of Leo XIII (1878–1903).

1985   Documents opened from the pontificates of Pius X (1903–14) and Benedict XV (1914–22).

2002   Pope John Paul II took the extraordinary step of making available, beginning in 2003, some of the documents from the Historical Archives of the Secretariat of State (Second Section), which pertain to the Vatican's relations with Germany during pontificate of Pius XI (1922–39).

JUNE   Pope Benedict XVI authorized opening of all the Vatican Archives for
2006   the pontificate of Pope Pius XI.

The Popes

This list is from New Advent, "The List of Popes" at www.newadvent.org/cathen/12272.html.

1. St. Peter (32–67)
2. St. Linus (67–76)
3. St. Anacletus (Cletus) (76–88)
4. St. Clement I (88–97)
5. St. Evaristus (97–105)
6. St. Alexander I (105–15)
7. St. Sixtus I (115–25) Also called Xystus I
8. St. Telesphorus (125–36)
9. St. Hyginus (136–40)
10. St. Pius I (140–55)
11. St. Anicetus (155–66)
12. St. Soter (166–75)
13. St. Eleutherius (175–89)
14. St. Victor I (189–99)
15. St. Zephyrinus (199–217)
16. St. Callistus I (217–22)
17. St. Urban I (222–30)
18. St. Pontain (230–35)
19. St. Anterus (235–36)
20. St. Fabian (236–50)
21. St. Cornelius (251–53)
22. St. Lucius I (253–54)
23. St. Stephen I (254–57)
24. St. Sixtus II (257–58)

25. St. Dionysius (260–68)
26. St. Felix I (269–74)
27. St. Eutychian (275–83)
28. St. Caius (283–96) Also called Gaius
29. St. Marcellinus (296–304)
30. St. Marcellus I (308–09)
31. St. Eusebius (309 or 310)
32. St. Miltiades (311–14)
33. St. Sylvester I (314–35)
34. St. Marcus (336)
35. St. Julius I (337–52)
36. Liberius (352–66)
37. St. Damasus I (366–83)
38. St. Siricius (384–99)
39. St. Anastasius I (399–401)
40. St. Innocent I (401–17)
41. St. Zosimus (417–18)
42. St. Boniface I (418–22)
43. St. Celestine I (422–32)
44. St. Sixtus III (432–40)
45. St. Leo I (the Great) (440–61)
46. St. Hilarius (461–68)
47. St. Simplicius (468–83)
48. St. Felix III (II) (483–92)
49. St. Gelasius I (492–96)
50. Anastasius II (496–98)
51. St. Symmachus (498–514)
52. St. Hormisdas (514–23)
53. St. John I (523–26)
54. St. Felix IV (III) (526–30)
55. Boniface II (530–32)
56. John II (533–35)
57. St. Agapetus I (535–36) Also called Agapitus I

58. St. Silverius (536–37)
59. Vigilius (537–55)
60. Pelagius I (556–61)
61. John III (561–74)
62. Benedict I (575–79)
63. Pelagius II (579–90)
64. St. Gregory I (the Great) (590–604)
65. Sabinian (604–06)
66. Boniface III (607)
67. St. Boniface IV (608–15)
68. St. Deusdedit (Adeodatus I) (615–18)
69. Boniface V (619–25)
70. Honorius I (625–38)
71. Severinus (640)
72. John IV (640–42)
73. Theodore I (642–49)
74. St. Martin I (649–55)
75. St. Eugene I (655–57)
76. St. Vitalian (657–72)
77. Adeodatus (II) (672–76)
78. Donus (676–78)
79. St. Agatho (678–81)
80. St. Leo II (682–83)
81. St. Benedict II (684–85)
82. John V (685–86)
83. Conon (686–87)
84. St. Sergius I (687–701)
85. John VI (701–05)
86. John VII (705–07)
87. Sisinnius (708)
88. Constantine (708–15)
89. St. Gregory II (715–31)
90. St. Gregory III (731–41)

91. St. Zachary (741–52)
92. Stephen II (752)
93. Stephen III (752–57)
94. St. Paul I (757–67)
95. Stephen IV (767–72)
96. Adrian I (772–95)
97. St. Leo III (795–816)
98. Stephen V (816–17)
99. St. Paschal I (817–24)
100. Eugene II (824–27)
101. Valentine (827)
102. Gregory IV (827–44)
103. Sergius II (844–47)
104. St. Leo IV (847–55)
105. Benedict III (855–58)
106. St. Nicholas I (the Great) (858–67)
107. Adrian II (867–72)
108. John VIII (872–82)
109. Marinus I (882–84)
110. St. Adrian III (884–85)
111. Stephen VI (885–91)
112. Formosus (891–96)
113. Boniface VI (896)
114. Stephen VII (896–97)
115. Romanus (897)
116. Theodore II (897)
117. John IX (898-900)
118. Benedict IV (900–03)
119. Leo V (903)
120. Sergius III (904–11)
121. Anastasius III (911–13)
122. Lando (913–14)
123. John X (914–28)

124. Leo VI (928)
125. Stephen VIII (929–31)
126. John XI (931–35)
127. Leo VII (936–39)
128. Stephen IX (939–42)
129. Marinus II (942–46)
130. Agapetus II (946–55)
131. John XII (955–63)
132. Leo VIII (963–64)
133. Benedict V (964)
134. John XIII (965–72)
135. Benedict VI (973–74)
136. Benedict VII (974–83)
137. John XIV (983–84)
138. John XV (985–96)
139. Gregory V (996–99)
140. Sylvester II (999–1003)
141. John XVII (1003)
142. John XVIII (1003–09)
143. Sergius IV (1009–12)
144. Benedict VIII (1012–24)
145. John XIX (1024–32)
146. Benedict IX (1032–45)
147. Sylvester III (1045)
148. Benedict IX (1045)
149. Gregory VI (1045–46)
150. Clement II (1046–47)
151. Benedict IX (1047–48)
152. Damasus II (1048)
153. St. Leo IX (1049–54)
154. Victor II (1055–57)
155. Stephen X (1057–58)
156. Nicholas II (1058–61)

157. Alexander II (1061–73)

158. St. Gregory VII (1073–85)

159. Blessed Victor III (1086–87)

160. Blessed Urban II (1088–99)

161. Paschal II (1099–1118)

162. Gelasius II (1118–19)

163. Callistus II (1119–24)

164. Honorius II (1124–30)

165. Innocent II (1130–43)

166. Celestine II (1143–44)

167. Lucius II (1144–45)

168. Blessed Eugene III (1145–53)

169. Anastasius IV (1153–54)

170. Adrian IV (1154–59)

171. Alexander III (1159–81)

172. Lucius III (1181–85)

173. Urban III (1185–87)

174. Gregory VIII (1187)

175. Clement III (1187–91)

176. Celestine III (1191–98)

177. Innocent III (1198–1216)

178. Honorius III (1216–27)

179. Gregory IX (1227–41)

180. Celestine IV (1241)

181. Innocent IV (1243–54)

182. Alexander IV (1254–61)

183. Urban IV (1261–64)

184. Clement IV (1265–68)

185. Blessed Gregory X (1271–76)

186. Blessed Innocent V (1276)

187. Adrian V (1276)

188. John XXI (1276–77)

189. Nicholas III (1277–80)

190. Martin IV (1281–85)
191. Honorius IV (1285–87)
192. Nicholas IV (1288–92)
193. St. Celestine V (1294)
194. Boniface VIII (1294–1303)
195. Blessed Benedict XI (1303–04)
196. Clement V (1305–14)
197. John XXII (1316–34)
198. Benedict XII (1334–42)
199. Clement VI (1342–52)
200. Innocent VI (1352–62)
201. Blessed Urban V (1362–70)
202. Gregory XI (1370–78)
203. Urban VI (1378–89)
204. Boniface IX (1389–1404)
205. Innocent VII (1406–06)
206. Gregory XII (1406–15)
207. Martin V (1417–31)
208. Eugene IV (1431–47)
209. Nicholas V (1447–55)
210. Callistus III (1455-58)
211. Pius II (1458–64)
212. Paul II (1464–71)
213. Sixtus IV (1471–84)
214. Innocent VIII (1484–92)
215. Alexander VI (1492–1503)
216. Pius III (1503)
217. Julius II (1503–13)
218. Leo X (1513–21)
219. Adrian VI (1522–23)
220. Clement VII (1523–34)
221. Paul III (1534–49)
222. Julius III (1550–55)

223. Marcellus II (1555)
224. Paul IV (1555–59)
225. Pius IV (1559–65)
226. St. Pius V (1566–72)
227. Gregory XIII (1572–85)
228. Sixtus V (1585–90)
229. Urban VII (1590)
230. Gregory XIV (1590–91)
231. Innocent IX (1591)
232. Clement VIII (1592–1605)
233. Leo XI (1605)
234. Paul V (1605–21)
235. Gregory XV (1621–23)
236. Urban VIII (1623–44)
237. Innocent X (1644–55)
238. Alexander VII (1655–67)
239. Clement IX (1667–69)
240. Clement X (1670–76)
241. Blessed Innocent XI (1676–89)
242. Alexander VIII (1689–91)
243. Innocent XII (1691–1700)
244. Clement XI (1700–21)
245. Innocent XIII (1721–24)
246. Benedict XIII (1724–30)
247. Clement XII (1730–40)
248. Benedict XIV (1740–58)
249. Clement XIII (1758–69)
250. Clement XIV (1769–74)
251. Pius VI (1775–99)
252. Pius VII (1800–23)
253. Leo XII (1823–29)
254. Pius VIII (1829–30)
255. Gregory XVI (1831–46)
256. Blessed Pius IX (1846–78)

257. Leo XIII (1878–1903)
258. St. Pius X (1903–14)
259. Benedict XV (1914–22)
260. Pius XI (1922–39)
261. Pius XII (1939–58)
262. Blessed John XXIII (1958–63)
263. Paul VI (1963–78)
264. John Paul I (1978)
265. John Paul II (1978–2005)
266. Benedict XVI (2005–)

Chinon Parchment

The Chinon Parchment is from In Rebus, "The Chinon Parchment: Were the Knights Pardoned?" at www.inrebus.com/chinon.php.

In the name of the Lord, amen. We, Berengar, by the mercy of God cardinal presbyter of SS. Nereus and Achileus, and Stephanus, cardinal presbyter of St. Ciriacus in Therminis, and Landolf, cardinal deacon of St. Angel, declare through this official statement directed to all who will read it that since our most holy father and lord Clement, by divine providence the supreme pontific of the holy Roman and universal church, after receiving the word of mouth and also clamorous reports from the illustrious king of France and prelates, dukes, counts, barons and other subjects of the said kingdom, both noblemen and commoners, along with some brothers, presbyters, knights, preceptors and servants of the Templar Order, had initiated an inquiry into matters concerning the brothers, [questions of Catholic faith] and the Rule of the said Order, because of which it suffered public infamy, the very same lord Pope wishing and intending to know the pure, complete and uncompromised truth from the leaders of the said Order, namely brother Jacques de Molay, grandmaster of the Order of Knights Templar, brother Raymbaud de Caron, preceptor the commandaries of Templar Knights in Outremer, brother Hugo de Pérraud, preceptor of France, brother Geoffroy de Gonneville, preceptor of Aquitania and Poitou, and Geoffroy of Charny, preceptor of Normandy, ordered and commissioned us specifically and by his verbally expressed will in order that we might with diligence examine the truth by questioning the grandmaster and the aforementioned preceptors—one by one and individually, having summoned notaries public and trust-worthy witnesses.

And having acted according to the mandate and commissioned by the said Lord Supreme Pontific, we questioned the aforementioned grand-master and the preceptors and examined them concerning the matters described above. Their words and confessions were written down exactly the way they are included here by the notaries whose names are listed below in the presence of witnesses listed below. We also ordered these things drawn up in this official form and validated by the protection of our seals.

In the year of our Lord 1308, the 6th indiction, on the 17th day of August, in the 3d year of the pontificate of the said Pope Clement V, brother Raymbaud de Caron, preceptor the commandaries of Templar Knights in *Outremer*, was brought in front of us, the aforementioned fathers, to the town of Chinon of the Tours diocese. With his hand on the Holy Gospel of the Lord he took an oath that he would speak pure and complete truth about himself as well [as] individuals and brothers of the Order, and about the Order itself, concerning questions of Catholic faith and the Rule of the said Order, and also about five particular individuals and brothers of the Order. Diligently interrogated by us about the time and circumstances of his initiation in the Order he said that it has been forty-three years or thereabouts since he had been knighted and admitted into the Templar Order by brother Roncelin de Fos, at the time preceptor of Provence, in the town of Richarenchess, in the diocese of Carpentras or Saint-Paul-Trois-Châteaux, in the chapel of the local Templar commandery. During the ceremony the patron said nothing to the novice that was not proper, but after the admittance a servant-brother came up to him whose name he does not recall, for he has been dead for a long time. He took him aside holding a small cross under his cloak, and when all the brothers exited and they remained alone, that is this brother-servant and the speaker, this brother-servant showed this cross to the speaker who does not recall whether it bore the effigy of the crucifix or not, but believes however, that there was a crucifix either painted or carved. And this brother-servant told the speaker: "You must denounce this one." And the speaker, not believing himself to be committing a sin, said: "And so, I denounce." That brother-servant also told the speaker that he should preserve purity and chastity, but if he could not do so, it was better to be done secretly than publicly. The speaker also said that his denunciation did not come from the heart, but from the mouth. Then he said that the next day he revealed this to the bishop of Carpentras, his blood relative, who was present in the said place, and the bishop told him that he had acted wrongly and committed a sin. Then the interrogated confessed on this account to the same bishop and was assigned penances which he completed, according to him.

When asked about the sin of sodomy, he said that he never was a part of it neither performing or enduring, and that he never heard that Knights Templar engaged in this sin, apart from those three knights who had been punished by perpetual incarceration in Castle Pilgrim. When asked whether the brothers of the said Order were received into the Order in the same manner he was received into it, he replied that he did not know that, because he never initiated anyone himself and did not see anyone being accepted in the Order other than two or three brothers. Regarding them he did not know whether they denounced Christ or not. When he was asked about the names of these brothers he said that one had the name of Peter, but that he did not remember his family name. When he was asked how old he was when he was made brother of the said Order he replied that he was seventeen years of age or thereabouts. When he was asked about the spitting on the cross and about the worshipped head, he said that he knew nothing, adding that he had never heard any mention of that head until he heard the lord Pope Clement speak of it this past year. When he was asked about the practice of kissing, he replied that the aforementioned brother Roncelin kissed him on the mouth when he received him as a brother; he said that he knew nothing about other kisses. When he was asked whether he wanted to maintain what he had said during the confession, whether it was done according to the truth, and whether he had added anything untruthful or withheld anything that is truthful, he replied that he wanted to maintain what he had previously said in his confession, that it was truthful and that he neither added anything that was untruthful nor omitted anything that was truthful. When he was asked whether he had confessed due to a request, reward, gratitude, favor, fear, hatred or persuasion by someone else, or the use of force, or fear of impending torture, he replied that he did not.

Afterwards, this very brother Raymbaud standing on his knees with his hands folded asked for our forgiveness and mercy regarding the above-mentioned deeds. And as he pleaded so, brother Raymbaud denounced in our presence the above-mentioned heresy, as well as any other heresy. For the second time he took an oath with his hand upon the Holy Gospel of our Lord in that he will obey the teachings of the Church, that he will maintain, uphold and observe the Catholic faith which the Roman Church maintains, upholds and proclaims, as well as teaches and requires of others to observe it, and that he will live and die as a faithful Christian. After this oath, by the authority of lord Pope specifically granted to us for that purpose, we extended to this humbly asking brother Raymbaud, in a form accepted by the Church the mercy of absolution from the verdict of excommunication that had been incurred by the aforementioned deeds, restoring him to unity with the Church and reinstating him for communion of the faithful and sacraments of the Church.

Also, on the same day, brother knight Geoffroy of Charny, preceptor of commanderies of the Templar Order in Normandy, appearing personally in the previously described manner and form, in our presence, and in the presence of notaries, as well as witnesses, modestly swore with his hand on the Gospel of the Lord and was questioned about the manner of his reception into the said Order. He testified that it has well been forty years or thereabouts since he was accepted into the Order of Knights Templar by brother Amaury de la Roche, the preceptor of France in Étamps of the diocese of Sens, in the chapel of the local Templar commandery. Present at the ceremony were brother Jean le Franceys, preceptor of Pédenac, and nine, ten or so brothers of the said Order whom he all believed to be dead now. And then, once he had been accepted in the Order and the cloak of the Order had been placed on his shoulders, the brother who performed the ceremony took him aside within the same chapel and showed him a crucifix with an effigy of Christ, and told him that he should not believe in the Crucified, but should in fact denounce Him. Then the newly accepted brother at the demand of the said recipient denounced Him verbally, but not in his heart. Also, he said that at the time of his induction, the novice kissed the recipient on the mouth and in his chest through the garment as a sign of reverence.

When asked whether brothers of the Templar Order while being initiated into the Order were accepted in the same manner that he was, he said that he did not know. He also said that he himself received one brother into the said Order through the same ceremony through which he himself was accepted. Afterwards he accepted many others without the denunciation described earlier and in good manner. He also said that he confessed about the denunciation of the cross which he had done during the ceremony of induction and about being forced to do so by the brother performing the ceremony, to the Patriarch of Jerusalem of the time, and was absolved by him.

When diligently questioned regarding the spitting on the cross, the practice of kissing, the vice of sodomy and the worshipped head, he replied that he knew nothing of it. Further interrogated, he said that he believed that other brothers had been accepted into the Order in the same manner that he was. He said however that he did not know that for sure since when these things took place the newly received were taken aside so that other brothers who were present in the building would neither see nor hear what went on with them. Asked about the age that he was in when accepted into the said Order, he replied that he was sixteen, seventeen or thereabouts.

When he was asked whether he had said these things due to a request, reward, gratitude, favor, fear, hatred or persuasion by someone else, or the use of force, or fear of impending torture, he replied that he did not. When he was asked whether he wanted to maintain what he had said during the confession, whether it was done according to the truth, and whether he had added anything untruthful or withheld anything that was truthful, he replied that he wanted to maintain what he had previously said in his confession during which he had only said what was true, that what he said was according to the truth and that he neither added anything that was untruthful nor omitted anything that was truthful.

After this, we concluded to extend the mercy of absolution for these acts to brother Geoffroy, who in the form and manner described above had denounced in our presence the described and any other heresy, and swore in person on the Lord's Holy Gospel, and humbly asked for the mercy of absolution, restoring him to unity with the Church and reinstating him for communion of the faithful and sacraments of the Church.

On the same day, in our presence and the presence of notaries, as well as the witnesses listed below, brother Geoffroy de Gonneville personally appeared and was diligently questioned about the time and circumstances of his reception and about other matters described above. He replied that it has been twenty-eight years or thereabouts since he was received as a brother of the Order of the Knights Templar by brother-knight Robert de Torville, preceptor of the commandaries of the Templar Order in England, in the city of London, at the chapel of the local commandery. And this receptor, after bestowing the cloak of the Knights Templar upon the newly received member, showed him the cross depicted in some book and said that he should denounce the one whose image was depicted on that cross. When the newly received did not want to do so, the receptor told him multiple times that he should do so. And since he completely refused to do it, the receptor, seeing his resistance, said to him: "Will you swear to me that if asked by any of the brothers you would say that you had made this denouncement, provided that I allow you not to make it?" And the newly received answered "yes," and promised that if he was questioned by any of the brothers of the said Order he would say that he had performed the said denouncement. And, as he said, he made no denouncement otherwise. He also said that the said receptor told him that he should spit on the described cross. When the newly received did not wish to do so, the receptor placed his own hand over the depiction of the cross and said: "At least spit on my hand!" And since the received feared that the receptor would remove his hand and some of this spit would get on the cross, he did not want to spit on the hand with the cross being near.

When diligently questioned regarding the sin of sodomy, the worshipped head, about the practice of kissing and other things for which the brothers of the said Order received a bad reputation, he said that he knew nothing. When asked whether other brothers of the Order were accepted into the Order in the same way as he was, he said that he believed that the same was done to others as it was done to him at the time of his described initiation.

When he was asked whether he had said these things due to a request, reward, gratitude, favor, fear, hatred or persuasion by someone else, or the use of force, or fear of impending torture, he replied that he did not. After this, we concluded to extend the mercy of absolution for these acts to brother Geoffroy de Gonneville, who in the form and manner described above had denounced in our presence the described and any other heresy, and swore in person on the Lord's Holy Gospel, and humbly asked for the mercy of absolution, restoring him to unity with the Church and reinstating him for communion of the faithful and sacraments of the Church.

Then on the nineteenth day of the month, in our presence, and in the presence of notaries and the same witnesses, brother Hugo de Pérraud, preceptor of Templar commanderies in France appeared personally and took an oath on the Holy Gospel of the Lord, placing his hand upon it in the manner described above. This brother Hugo, having sworn as indicated, and being diligently questioned said about the manner of his initiation that he was received in London at the local Templar commandary, in its church. It was forty-six years ago this past feast of St. Magdalene. He was inducted as a brother of the Order by brother Hubet de Pérraud, his own father, a Visitator of the Templar commanderies in France and Poitou, who placed upon his shoulders the cloak of the said Order. This having been done, some brother of the said Order, by the name of John, who afterwards became preceptor of de La Muce, took him to a certain part of that chapel, showed him a cross with an effigy of Christ, and ordered him to denounce the One whose image was depicted there. He refused, as much as he could, according to him. Eventually, however, overcome by fear and menaces of brother John, he denounced the One whose image was depicted there only once. And although brother John multiple times demanded that he spit on that cross, he refused to do so.

When asked whether he had to kiss the receptor, he said that he did, only on the mouth.

When asked about the sin of sodomy, he replied that it was never imposed on him and he never committed it.

When asked whether he accepted others into the Order, he replied that he did many times, and that he accepted more people than any other living member of the Order.

When asked about the ceremony through which he accepted them, he said that after they were received and given the cloaks of the Order, he ordered them to denounce the crucifix and to kiss him at the bottom of the back, in the navel and then on the mouth. He also said that he imposed on them to abstain from partnership with women, and, if they were unable to restrain their lust, to join themselves with brothers of the Order.

He also said under oath that the aforementioned denunciation, which he performed during initiation, as well as other things described that he demanded from those received by him, was done in word only, and not in spirit. When asked why he felt pained and did not perform in spirit the things that he did, he replied that such were the statutes or rather traditions of the Order and that he always hoped that this error would be removed from the said Order.

When asked whether any of the members newly received by him refused to perform the described spitting and other dishonest things listed above, he replied that only few, and eventually all did as ordered. He also said that although he himself instructed brothers of the Order whom he initiated to join with other brothers, nevertheless he never did that, nor heard that anyone else committed this sin, except for the two or three brothers in Outremer who were incarcerated for this in Castle Pilgrim.

When asked whether he knew if all brothers of the said Order were initiated in the same manner as he initiated others, he said that he did not know for sure about others, only about himself and those whom he initiated, because brothers are initiated in such secrecy that nothing can be known other than through those who are present. When asked whether he believed that they were all initiated in this manner, he said that he believed that the same ritual was used while initiating others as it was used in his case and as he himself administered when he received others.

When asked about the head of an idol that was reportedly worshipped by the Templars, he said that it was shown to him in Montpellier by brother Peter Alemandin, preceptor of that place, and that this head remained in possession of brother Peter.

When asked how old he was when accepted into the said Order, he replied that he heard his mother say that he was eighteen. He also said that previously he had confessed about these things in the presence of brother Guillaume of Paris, inquisitor of heretical actions, or his deputy. This confession was written down in the hand of the undersigning Amise d'Orleans and some other notaries public. He wishes to maintain that confession, just as it is, as well as maintain in the present confession that which is in concord with the previous one. And if there is anything additional in this confession in front of the Inquisitor or his deputy, as has been said above, he ratifies, approves and confirms it.

When he was asked whether he had confessed to these things due to a request, reward, gratitude, favor, fear, hatred or persuasion by someone else, or the use of force, or fear of impending torture, he replied that he did not. When he was asked whether he, after being apprehended, was submitted to any questioning or torture, he replied that he was not.

After this, we concluded to extend the mercy of absolution for these acts to brother Hugo, who in the form and manner described above had denounced in our presence the described and any other heresy, and swore in person on the Lord's Holy Gospel, and humbly asked for the mercy of absolution, restoring him to unity with the Church and reinstating him to communion of the faithful and sacraments of the Church.

Then on the twentieth day of the month, in our presence, and in the presence of notaries and the same witnesses, brother-knight Jacques de Molay, grandmaster of the Order of Knights Templar appeared personally and having sworn in the form and manner indicated above, and having been diligently questioned, said it had been forty-two years or thereabouts since he was received as a brother of the said Order by brother-knight Hubert de Pérraud, at the time Visitator of France and Poitou, in Beune, diocese of Autun, in the chapel of the local Templar commandery of that place.

Concerning the way of his initiation into the Order, he said that having given him the cloak, the receptor showed to him <the cross> and told him that he should denounce the God whose image was depicted on that cross, and that he should spit on the cross. Which he did, although he did not spit on the cross, [but] near it, according to his words. He also said that he performed this denunciation in words, not in spirit. Regarding the sin of sodomy, the worshipped head and the practice of illicit kisses, he, diligently questioned, said that he knew nothing of that.

When he was asked whether he had confessed to these things due to a request, reward, gratitude, favor, fear, hatred or persuasion by someone else, or the use of force, or fear of impending torture, he replied that he was not. When he was asked whether he, after being apprehended, was submitted to any questioning or torture, he replied that he was not.

After this, we concluded to extend the mercy of absolution for these acts to brother Jacques de Molay, the grandmaster of the said Order, who in the form and manner described above had denounced in our presence the described and any other heresy, and swore in person on the Lord's Holy Gospel, and humbly asked for the mercy of absolution, restoring him to unity with the Church and reinstating him to communion of the faithful and sacraments of the Church.

On the same twentieth day of the month, in our presence, and in the presence of notaries and the same witnesses, brother Geoffroy de Gonneville freely and willingly ratified, approved and confirmed his signed confession that was read to him in his native tongue, and gave assurances that he intended to stand by and maintain both this confession and the confession he made on a different occasion in front of the Inquisitor or inquisitors regarding the aforementioned heretic transgressions, in as much as it was in concordance with the confession made in front of us, the notaries and the aforementioned witnesses; and that if there is something extra contained in the confession made in front of the Inquisitor and inquisitors, as it was said earlier, he ratifies, approves and confirms that.

On the same twentieth day of the month, in our presence, and in the presence of notaries and the same witnesses, brother-preceptor Hugo de Pérraud in a similar way freely and willingly ratified, approved and confirmed his signed confession that was read to him in his native tongue.

We ordered Robert de Condet, cleric of the diocese of Soissons, a notary by apostolic power, who was among us together with notaries and witnesses listed below, to record and make public as evidence these confessions, as well as each and every thing described above that occurred in front of us, the notaries and the witnesses, and also everything done by us, exactly as it is shown above, and to validate it by attaching our seal.

This was done on the year, indiction, month, day, pontificate and the place indicated above, in our presence and the presence of Umberto Vercellani, Nicolo Nicolai de Benvenuto and the aforementioned Robert de Condet, and also master Amise d'Orleans le Ratif, notaries public by the apostolic power, as well as pious and distinguished brother Raymond, abbot of the Benedictine monastery of St. Theofred, Annecy diocese, master Berard de Boiano, archdeacon of Troia, Raoul de Boset, confessor and canon from Paris, and Pierre de Soire, overseer of Saint-Gaugery in Cambresis, who were gathered specifically as witnesses.

And I, Robert de Condet, cleric of the diocese of Soissons, notary by apostolic power, observed with other notaries and witnesses each and every thing described above that occurred in the presence of the aforementioned reverend fathers lords cardinal presbyters, myself and other notaries and witnesses, as well as what was done by their lordships. On the orders from their lordships the cardinal presbyters, I made this record, and put in the official form, and sealed it with my seal, having been asked to do so.

And also I, Umberto Vercellani, cleric of Béziers, notary by apostolic power, observed with other notaries and witnesses each and every thing described above that occurred in the presence of the aforementioned lords cardinal presbyters, as well as what was done by their lordships cardinal presbyters just as it is shown above in fuller detail. On the orders from these cardinal presbyters, for further assurance, I wrote underneath this record and sealed it with my seal.

And also I, Nicolo Nicolai di Benevento, notary by apostolic decree, observed with other aforementioned notaries and witnesses each and every thing described above that occurred in the presence of the aforementioned lords cardinal presbyters, as well as what was done by their lordships just as it is shown above in fuller detail. On the orders from these cardinal presbyters, for further assurance, I wrote underneath this record and sealed it with my seal.

And also I, Arnulphe d'Orléans called le Ratif, notary by the power of the Holy Roman Church, observed with other aforementioned notaries and witnesses confessions, depositions and other each and every thing described above that occurred in the presence of the aforementioned reverend fathers lords cardinal presbyters, as well as what was done by their lordships just as it is shown above in fuller detail. On the orders from these cardinal presbyters, as a testimony of truth, I wrote underneath this record and sealed it with my seal, having been asked to do so.

The Lateran Treaty of 1929
(excerpts)

Excerpts from the Lateran Treaty of 1929 are from
spcp.prf.cuni.cz/dokument/lateran.htm.

Whereas the Holy See and Italy have recognized the desirability of eliminating every reason for dissension existing between them and arriving at a final settlement of their reciprocal relations which shall be consistent with justice and with the dignity of both High Contracting Parties, and which by permanently assuring to the Holy See a position *de facto* and *de jure* which shall guarantee absolute independence for the fulfillment of its exalted mission in the world, permits the Holy See to consider as finally and irrevocably settled the Roman Question which arose in 1870 by the annexation of Rome to the Kingdom of Italy, under the Dynasty of the House of Savoy;

And whereas it was obligatory, for the purpose of assuring the absolute and visible independence of the Holy See, likewise to guarantee its indisputable sovereignty in international matters, it has been found necessary to create under special conditions the Vatican City, recognizing the full ownership, exclusive and absolute dominion and sovereign jurisdiction of the Holy See over that City;

His Holiness the Supreme Pontiff Pius XI and His Majesty Victor Emanuel III, King of Italy, have agreed to conclude a Treaty, appointing for that purpose two Plenipotentiaries, being on behalf of His Holiness, His Secretary of State, viz. His Most Reverend Eminence the Lord Cardinal Pietro Gasparri, and on behalf of his Majesty, His Excellency the Cav. Benito Mussolini, Prime Minister and Head of the Government; who, having exchanged their respective full powers, which were found to be in due and proper form, have hereby agreed to the following articles:

Article 1

Italy recognizes and reaffirms the principle established in the first Article of the Italian Constitution dated March 4, 1848, according to which the Catholic Apostolic Roman religion is the only State religion.

Article 2

Italy recognizes the sovereignty of the Holy See in international matters as an inherent attribute in conformity with its traditions and the requirements of its mission to the world.

Article 3

Italy recognizes the full ownership, exclusive dominion, and sovereign authority and jurisdiction of the Holy See over the Vatican as at present constituted, together with all its appurtenances and endowments, thus creating the Vatican City, for the special purposes and under the conditions hereinafter referred to.

It is furthermore agreed that, although forming part of the Vatican City, St. Peter's Square shall continue to be normally open to the public and shall be subject to supervision by the Italian police authorities, which powers shall cease to operate at the foot of the steps leading to the Basilica, although the latter shall continue to be used for public worship. The said authorities shall, therefore, abstain from mounting the steps and entering the said Basilica, unless and except they are requested to do so by the proper authorities.

Should the Holy See consider it necessary, for the purpose of special ceremonies, temporarily to prohibit the public from free access to St. Peter's Square, the Italian authorities shall (unless specially requested to do otherwise) withdraw to beyond the outer lines of Bernini's Colonnade and the extension thereof.

Article 4

The sovereignty and exclusive jurisdiction over the Vatican City, which Italy recognizes as appertaining to the Holy See, forbid any intervention therein on the part of the Italian Government, or that any authority other than that of the Holy See shall be there acknowledged.

. . .

Article 7

The Italian Government undertakes to prohibit the construction within the territory surrounding the Vatican City, of any new buildings which might overlook the latter, and shall for a like purpose provide for the partial demolition of similar buildings already standing....

In accordance with the provisions of International Law, it shall be forbidden for aircraft of any kind whatsoever to fly over Vatican territory.

Article 8

Considering the person of the Supreme Pontiff to be sacred and inviolable, Italy declares any attempt against His person or any incitement to commit such attempt to be punishable by the same penalties as all similar attempts and incitements to commit the same against the person of the King.

All offences or public insults committed within Italian territory against the person of the Supreme Pontiff, whether by means of speeches, acts, or writings, shall be punished in the same manner as offences and insults against the person of the King.

Article 9

In accordance with the provisions of International Law, all persons having a permanent residence within the Vatican City shall be subject to the sovereignty of the Holy See. Such residence shall not be forfeited by reason of the mere fact of temporary residence elsewhere, unaccompanied by the loss of habitation in the said City or other circumstances proving that such residence has been abandoned.

Article 11

All central bodies of the Catholic Church shall be exempt from any interference on the part of the Italian State (save and except as provided by Italian law in regard to the acquisition of property made by *corpi morali* [recognized public bodies], and with regard to the conversion of real estate).

Article 12

It is understood that Italy undertakes in all cases to allow the freedom of correspondence for all States, including belligerents, to and from the Holy See, as well as free access to the Apostolic See by Bishops from all over the world.

The High Contracting Parties undertake to establish normal diplomatic relations between each other, by accrediting an Italian Ambassador to the Holy See and a Papal Nuncio to Italy, who shall be the *doyen* of the Diplomatic Corps, in accordance with the ordinary practice recognized by the Congress of Vienna by the Act of June 9, 1815, in consequence of the sovereignty hereby recognized and without prejudice to the provisions of Article 19 hereof, the diplomats accredited by the Holy See and the diplomatic couriers dispatched in the name of the Supreme Pontiff, shall enjoy within Italian territory, even in time of war, the same treatment as that enjoyed by diplomatic personages and couriers of other foreign Governments, according to the provisions of International Law.

Article 13

Italy recognizes the full ownership of the Holy See over the patriarchal Basilicas of St. John Lateran, Sta. Maria Maggiore, and St. Paul, with their annexed buildings.

The State transfers to the Holy See the free management and administration of the said Basilica of St. Paul and its dependent Monastery, also paying over to the Holy See all monies representing the sums set aside annually for that church in the budget of the Ministry of Education.

Article 14

Italy recognizes the full ownership by the Holy See of the Papal Palace of Castel Gandolfo, together with all endowments, appurtenances, and dependencies thereof, which are now already in the possession of the Holy See, and Italy also undertakes to hand over, within six months after the coming into force of the present Treaty, the Villa Barberini in Castel Gandolfo, together with all endowments, appurtenances, and dependencies thereof.

Further Reading

Aarons, Mark, and John Loftus. *Unholy Trinity: The Vatican, the Nazis and the Swiss Banks*. New York: St. Martin's Press, 1991.

Allen, John L. Jr. *All the Pope's Men: The Inside Story of How the Vatican Really Thinks*. New York: Doubleday, 2004.

———. *Opus Dei*. New York: Doubleday, 2005.

Amborsini, Maria Luisa, with Mary Willis. *The Secrets of the Vatican Archives*. New York: Barnes & Noble, 1996.

Baumgarten, Paul Maria. *The Vatican Library and Its Secret Archives*. Whitefish, MT: Kessinger, 2008.

Bander, Peter. *The Prophecies of St. Malachy & St. Columbkille*. Gerrards Cross, Buckinghamshire, UK: Collins Smythe, 1969.

Bokun, Branko. *Spy in the Vatican*. London: Tom Stacey, 1973.

Botting, Douglas, and Ian Sayer. *Nazi Gold*. New York: Grove Press, 1984.

Chadwick, Owen. *Catholicism and History: The Opening of the Vatican Archives*. Cambridge, England: Cambridge University Press, 1978.

Cheetham, Nicolas. *Keeper of the Keys: The Pope in History*. London: Macdonald, 1982.

Collins, Paul. *Papal Power*. London: HarperCollins, 1997.

Cornwell, John. *The Pontiff in Winter: Triumph and Conflict in the Reign of John Paul II*. New York: Doubleday, 2004.

———. *A Thief in the Night: The Death of John Paul I*. London: Viking, 1989.

Cornwell, Rupert. *God's Banker: The Life and Death of Roberto Calvi*. London: Unwin, 1984.

Doyle, Thomas P., A. W. R. Sipe, and Patrick J. Wall. *Sex, Priests and Codes: The Catholic Church's 2000-Year Paper Trail of Sexual Abuse*. Los Angeles: Volt Press, 2006.

Follain, John. *City of Secrets: The Startling Truth Behind the Vatican Murders*. New York: HarperCollins, 2004.

Friedlander, Saul. *Pius XII and the Third Reich*. London: Chatto & Windus, 1966.

Granfield, Patrick. *The Limits of the Papacy*. New York: Crossroads Books, 1987.

Greeley, Andrew. *The Making of the Popes*. London: Futura Press, 1978.

Gurwin. Larry. *The Calvi Affair: Death of a Banker*. London: Macmillan, 1983.

Jeffers, H. Paul. *Freemasons: Inside the World's Oldest Secret Society*. New York: Citadel Press, 2005.

Kelly. J. *The Oxford Dictionary of Popes*. Oxford, England: Oxford University Press, 1986.

Knight, Stephen. *The Brotherhood: The Secret World of the Fressmasons*. London: Granada, 1984.

Kung, Hans. *The Catholic Church: A Short History*. New York: The Modern Library, 2001.

Martin, Malachy. *The Vatican*. London: Secker & Warburg, 1986.

Murphy, Francis. *The Papacy Today*. New York: Macmillan, 1981.

Padallaro, Nazareno. *Portrait of Pius XII*. London: J. M. Dent, 1956.

Pallenberg, Corrado. *The Vatican from Within*. London: Harrap, 1961.

Podles, Leon J. *Sacrilege: Sexual Abuse in the Catholic Church*. Baltimore, MD: Crossland, 2008.

Poncins, Leon de. *Vatican and Freemasons*. Brooklyn, NY: Revisionist Press, 1982.

Shahrad, Cyrus. *Secrets of the Vatican*. New York: Gramercy, 2007.

Williams, Paul L. *The Vatican Exposed*. Amherst, NY: Prometheus, 2003.

Yallop, David. *In God's Name: An Investigation into the Murder of John Paul I*. New York: Carroll & Graf, 2007.

Index

Aarons, Mark, 92, 99
Act of Chinon, 19
Adrian III, Pope, 42
Agca, Mehmet Ali, 68–70, 108
Alessandrini, Emilio, 51
Alexander VI, Pope, 43, 128, 139
Algardi, Alessandro, 138–39
Allen, John, 80
Allen, Richard, 71, 72
Alvarez, David, 117–18
Amato, Angelo, 5–6
Ambrosioli, Giorgio, 52
America, the National Catholic Weekly, 6, 78, 86
Amorth, Gabriele, 123–24, 130
Anacletus, Pope, 34
Anderson, Jeffrey, 37
Andreev, Metodi, 70
Andreotti, Giulio, 123–24
Andropov, Yuri, 122
Angels & Demons (movie), 5, 6
Angleton, James Jesus, 66
Annotico Report, 55
Anrig, Daniel Rudolf, 116
Antonov, Sergei Ivanov, 69

Apostolic Library Museums, 26–27
Aquinas, Thomas, 33–34
Arcigay, 110–11
Arcudi, Giovanni, 114
Arzube, Juan, 37
Assets, 23–31
Attila the Hun, 138–39

Babic, Ivan, 102
Banco Ambrosiano, 48, 51–52, 55–58
Bank of Italy, 58
Barbie, Klaus, 98
Baronius, Cesare, 41
Barrajon, Pedro, 130
Basso, Michele, 28
Baumann, Paul, 80
Bayridge Residence, 76
Bellarmine, Robert, 11
Bellini, Federico, 141
Benedict III, Pope, 131
Benedict IX, Pope, 34, 43, 127
Benedict V, Pope, 43
Benedict VI, Pope, 42

Benedict XIV, Pope, 26, 36, 123
Benedict XV, Pope, 88, 132, 149, 153
Benedict XVI, Pope (Joseph Ratzinger), 149–50
  Fátima secret and, 146
  George W. Bush meeting with, 133
  on the Harry Potter novels, 14
  on Masonic associations, 21
  opening of the archives, 9–10, 153
  Opus Dei and, 81
  Pius XII and, 87
  St. Paul sarcophagus and, 137–38
  on sexual abuse, 39
  Swiss Guards and, 115–16
  Twisted Cross staff and, 130
Benigni, Umberto, 118
Berlusconi, Silvio, 59
Bernard, Saint, 148
Bernardin, Joseph, 76
Bernstein, Carl, 71–72
Berry, Jason, 37
Bertels, Ruth, 48
Biasetti, Mario, 111
Bible, approval of texts for inclusion, 1–2, 8
Bigelow, Pearson, 100–101
Birth control, 50
Blackfriars Bridge (London), 53–54
Blair, Tony, 133

Blech, Benjamin, 126–27
Blondel, David, 132
Blood Lies in the Vatican, 113–14
Boleyn, Anne, 3, 131
Bonavoglia, Angela, 38
Bonfante, Jordan, 44–45
Boniface VII, Pope, 34
Boniface VIII, Pope, 42
Book banning, 6–8, 12–14
Borgia, Cesare, 43, 139
Borgia, Lucrezia, 43, 139
Bormann, Martin, 119
Boyer, Leland, 37
Bramante, Donato, 140
Brossollet, Luc, 115
Brown, Dan, 3, 5–6, 14, 73, 74
Brunner, Alois, 100
Brunson, Matthew, 41–42
Buchs, Roland, 109, 111
Bush, George H.W., 66, 133
Bush, George W., 133–34
Bush, John Ellis "Jeb," 133

Callistus III, Pope, 139
Calo, Pippo, 59
Calvi, Carlo, 53–54
Calvi, Roberto, 48, 51–59, 93, 114
Calvin, John, 7
Canonization process, 77
Cappella Sistina (Sistine Chapel), 23–24, 27, 126–27
Carboni, Flavio, 58–59
Carlo-Stella, Maria Cristina, 140

Carter, Jimmy, 65, 133
Casaroli, Agostino, 71, 120
Casey, William, 66, 69–70
Castel Gandolfo, 30
Catanei, Vannoza, 43
Catherine of Aragon, 3, 131
Catholic News Agency (CNA), 83
Catholic World News, 124, 137
Chinon Parchment, 18–19, 22,
    165–76
Christianity, official recognition
    by Constantine of, 1–2
CIA (Central Intelligence
    Agency), 65–67, 69–70,
    96–97, 111
Cilice, 74
City of Secrets (Follain), 114–15
Clark, Mark W., 133
Clark, William, 71
Clement II, Pope, 42
Clement III, Pope, 148
Clement V, Pope, 3, 17–20, 128
Clement VI, Pope, 34
Clement VII, Pope, 34, 115
Clement XII, Pope, 55
Clement XIII, Pope, 26
Clement XIV, Pope, 41
Clinton, Bill, 133
Cody, John, 51
Congregation for Divine
    Worship, 124
Congregation for the Doctrine
    of the Faith, 6–7, 9, 56
Congregation of the Index, 7–8

Constantine, 1–2, 23, 136, 138
Copernicus, Nicholas, 10–12
Cornwell, John, 84–85
Corps of Gendarmerie of Vatican
    City, 115
Corriere della Sera, 70
Cosa Nostra (Mafia), 55–59,
    91–93
Council of Clermont, 15
Council of Nicaea, 1–2
Council of Troyes, 16
Council of Vienna, 19
Cova da Iria (Cove of Irene), 143
Crime of Solicitation, 33, 39
Croatia, 95–98, 100–104
Crusades, 15–16
Cusano, Nicolo, 136

Damasus II, Pope, 42
Darwin, Charles, 12
Da Silva, Jose, 145
Da Silva, Maria Candida, 144
DaVinci Code, The (Brown), 3,
    5–6, 8, 14, 73, 74
DaVinci Code, The (movie), 3,
    5–6, 73
*De Exorcismis et Supplicationibus
    Quibusdam (Of Exorcisms and
    Certain Supplications)*, 125
Defoe, Daniel, 8
Dellacha, Giuseppe, 52
Dell'Acqua, Angelo, 91
Del Monte, Innocenzo Ciocchi,
    127

De Luca, Maurizio, 28
De Mailly, Jean, 131
*De Modo Provedendi di Causis
    Crimine Soliciciones (On the
    Manner of Proceeding in Cases
    of the Crime of Solicitation)*,
    33, 39
De Molay, Jacques, 17, 19–20
Demonic possession, 123–26
De Paolis, Velasio, 5
De Payens, Hugues, 16
Deputy, The, a Christian Tragedy
    (play), 121–22
De Rosa, Peter, 43
D'Herbigny, Michael, 118
*Dialogue Concerning the Two Chief
    World Systems* (Galileo), 11
Di Carlo, Francesco, 59
DiFonzo, Luigi, 93
Diotallevi, Ernesto, 59
Discipline (cord-like whip), 74
Doliner, Roy, 126–27
Donovan, William, 66
Doomsday prophecies, 147–50
Doyle, Thomas, 37, 39
Draganovic, Krunoslav Stjepan,
    96–98, 100, 102
Durant, Will, 43
Dziwisz, Stanislaw, 68

Edict of Milan, 1
Eichmann, Adolf, 98, 100
Eisenhower, Dwight D., 133
Elling, George, 118

Elmbrook Student Center, 76
Entity, the, 117
Escrivá, Josemaría, 73–74, 76–78
Espionage, 66–67, 117–22
Estermann, Alois, 108–15, 117
Etsi Nos (On Conditions in Italy),
    55
Eugene IV, Pope, 9
Euphronius, 28
Evolution, 12
Exorcism, 123–26
Extraterrestrial life, 134–36
Ezekhial, 135–36

Fabbrica di San Pietro, 140–41
Farnese, Giulia, 43
Fátima, Portugal, 143–47
Ferigle, Sal, 75
Fessard, Gerald, 37
Fierz, Jacques-Antoine, 108,
    112–13
Filippi, Giorgio, 137
Finances, 23–31
First Things, 134
Flamini, Roland, 44–45
Fleetwood, Peter, 14
Flynn, Janice, 80
Follain, John, 114–15
Forbidden books, 6–8, 12–14
Fortune, 25
Foundations of National Socialism
    (Hudal), 99
Fourth Secret of Fatima (Socci),
    146–47

Foxman, Abraham, 94
Frale, Barbara, 18
Franco, Francisco, 73
Franklin National Bank of New York, 58
Frattini, Eric, 117
Freemasonry, 18, 20–22, 55–56
Freethought Today, 38
Friede, Johannes, 147
Fucci, Pietro, 114
Funes, José Gabriel, 134

Galileo Galilei, 3, 10–12
Gallagher, Charles R., 86–87
Gasparri, Pietro, 87–88
Gelli, Licio, 48, 50, 51, 59
Gennaro (Januarius), Saint, 92–93
Genovese, Vito, 93
Geocentrism, 11
George V of England, 88
Ginzburg, Carlo, 10
Gioia, Francesco, 137
Giordana, Mario, 28
Giuffrè, Antonino, 59
Godefroid (Geoffrey) de St. Omer, 16
Godfather, The (movies), 91, 94
Gold, 25, 30, 101–3
Goldstein, Laurie, 85–86
Good Catholic Girls (Bonavoglia), 38
Gowen, William, 102
Grab, Amédée, 112

Graham, Billy, 65
Graham, Robert, 100, 117–19
Gravity, and Galileo, 10
Gray Wolves, 69
Greeley, Andrew, 29–30
Green, Elizabeth W., 79
Gregory V, Pope, 42
Gregory IX, Pope, 9
Gregory XVI, Pope, 153
Grillini, Franco, 110–11
Gruner, Nicholas, 146
Gugel, Angelo, 68
Guicciardini, Francesco, 127
Gutenberg, Johann, 6

Haaretz, 102
Haig, Alexander, 66, 71
Hanssen, Robert, 78
Harry Potter novels, 14
Harvard University, 79
Heights School, 76
Henry IV of France, 138
Henry VIII of England, 3, 131
Heresy, 9–12
Heydrich, Reinhard, 119
Hitler, Adolf, 13–14, 83–86, 88–89, 107, 119, 122
Hitler's Pope (Cornwell), 84–85
Hochhuth, Rolf, 121–22
Holy Alliance, 117
Holy Cross Chapel, 76
Homosexuality, 33–34, 35, 38–39, 110–11, 114–15, 127, 132

Horobet, Gheorghe, 119–20
Howard, Ron, 5, 6
Hudal, Alois, 98–100
Humanum Genus, 20–21, 55–56

Il Messaggero, 110, 116
Il Quarto Segreto di Fatima
    (Socci), 146–47
Imperial Library, 9
Income, 25–26, 29, 30–31
Index Congregation, 7–8
Index Librorum Prohibitorum (The
    Index of Prohibited Books),
    6–8
In Eminenti Apostolatus, 55
Infessura, Stefano, 127
In God's Name (Yallop), 50–51,
    80–81
Innocent II, Pope, 148
Innocent III, Pope, 9, 128
Innocent VIII, Pope, 43
Inquisition, 9–13
International Association of
    Exorcists, 123
Into That Darkness (Sereny), 100
Ipekci, Abdi, 68
Istituto per le Opere di Religione
    (IOR). *See* Vatican Bank

Jablonski, Henryk, 62–63
Jagiellonian University, 61–62
Januarius, Saint (San Gennaro),
    92–93

Jesus Christ, 1, 130–31
Joan, Pope, 131–32
John of Patmos, 147
John Paul I, Pope, 44–52, 55, 149
John Paul II, Pope (Karol
    Wojtyła), 149, 153
    Agca assassination attempt,
        67–70, 108, 145–46
    Cardinal Stepinac and, 104
    demonic possession and,
        124–25
    election of, 51
    Fátima secret and, 145–46
    on Galileo, 12
    on the Harry Potter novels, 14
    on heresy, 13
    Opus Dei and, 73, 75, 76–77,
        80–81
    Pius XII and, 85, 87, 91
    Poland and Solidarity move-
        ment, 57, 59, 61–65, 71–72
    Reagan and, 65–72, 133
    Swiss Guards and, 112
    Twisted Cross staff and, 130
    UFOs and, 136
Johnson, Lyndon, 133
John VIII, Pope, 41, 42
John X, Pope, 42
John XII, Pope, 41, 42, 127
John XIII, Pope, 31
John XIV, Pope, 42
John XXIII, Pope, 26, 33, 36, 39,
    47, 133, 145

Julius II, Pope, 2, 23–24, 26, 43, 105, 106, 115
Julius III, Pope, 34, 127

Keating, Karl, 28–29
Kennedy, Joseph P., 86–87
Keys of This Blood, The (Martin), 129
KGB, 63–64, 69–71, 119–22
Khrushchev, Nikita, 119
Knights of Malta, 65–66
Knights Templar, 3, 15–22
Kuby, Gabriele, 14
Kvaternik, Eugen, 97

La Civiltá Cattolica (The Catholic Civilization), 118
Lady Chatterley's Lover (Lawrence), 8
La Repubblica, 133
Last Temptation of Christ, The (movie), 6
Lateran Treaty of 1929, 88, 92, 177–81
Leiber, Robert, 91
Leo I, Pope, 34, 43–44, 138–39
Leo IV, Pope, 131
Leo V, Pope, 42
Leo X, Pope, 127, 128
Leo XI, Pope, 138
Leo XIII, Pope, 3, 20–21, 55, 128, 152, 153
Leon, Donna, 91

Letter of Christ and Abgarus, 130–31
Lev, Elizabeth, 139
Levy, Jonathan, 102–3
Lexington College, 76
Licinius, 1
Lincoln Green Residence, 76
Livingston Masonic Library, 22
Lodge, Henry Cabot, Jr., 133
Loftus, John, 92, 99
Lombardi, Federico, 124
London Daily Telegraph, 20
London Guardian, 138
Lorenzi, Diego, 48
L'Osservatore Romano, 90–91, 134, 140
Luciano, Charles "Lucky," 93
Lucius III, Pope, 128
Ludwig III of Bavaria, 88
Luther, Martin, 7, 128
Luzi, Enrico Sini, 111

McAllister, Matthew, 80
McCrabb, Donald R., 78
Mäder, Elmar Theodor, 116
Madre di Deo (Mother of God), 124
Magee, John, 48
Magli, Ida, 110
Malachy, Saint, 148–50
Manhattan, Avro, 24–25
Marcinkus, Paul, 48, 51
Maria Laach Monastery, 147–48
Marquette University, 78–79

Marrone, Gianluigi, 114

Martin, James, 78

Martin, Malachi, 129–30

Marto, Francisco, 143–44

Marto, Jacinta, 143–45

Mary Magdalene, 3

Maxentius, 1

Mazzullo, Giuseppe, 122

Medina Estévez, Jorge Arturo, 124, 125–26

Mein Kampf (Hitler), 13–14

Meir, Golda, 90

Michelangelo Buonarotti, 3, 28, 107, 139–41

  Pietà, 27

  room at the Vatican ("Stanza di Michelangelo"), 140–41

  Sistine Chapel, 23–24, 27, 126–27

Milliyet, 68

Mit brennender Sorge (With Deep Anxiety), 84, 89

Montini, Giovanni Battista, 134

Montrose School, 76

Morlion, Felix, 66

Mountin, Susan, 78–79

Mueller, Heinrich, 98

Murders, 41–59, 105–16

Museo Pio-Clementino, 26

Mussolini, Benito, 30, 84, 92, 95, 99

Muzquiz, Joseph, 75

Myths and rumors, 129–34

Naples Cathedral, 92–93

Napoleon Bonaparte, 107

National Catholic Reporter, 80

National Review Online, 119

Navarro-Valls, Joaquin, 101, 110

Nazis (Nazism), 83–96, 98–100, 107, 118–22

Neuhaus, John, 134

New American, The, 130

Newsweek, 12–13, 77, 108, 110, 111, 112

New York Newsday, 80

New York Times, 36, 68, 85–86, 124–25, 146

Nicaean Creed, 1–2

Nicholas V, Pope, 2, 9, 151

Northridge Prep School, 76

Nothing Sacred (Alvarez), 117–18

Oakcrest School, 76

Of Exorcisms and Certain Supplications (De Exorcismis et Supplicationibus Quibusdam), 125

Oliveiro, Antonio de, 143

Opus Dei, 73–81, 105–6, 113–14

Opus Dei Awareness Network, 80

Origin of the Species, The (Darwin), 12

Orsenigo, Cesare, 118

Ortolani, Umberto, 48, 51

OSS (Office of Strategic Services), 66, 101

Ostpolitik des Vatikans, 118–19
Ottaviani, Alfredo, 33, 145
Our Lady of Fátima, 143–47
Owen, Mark, 42

Pacepa, Ion Mihai, 119–22
Palatine Library, 9
Papal Tiara, 131
Paul, Saint, 126, 137–38
Paul II, Pope, 34, 51, 133
Paul III, Pope, 43, 127–28, 140
Paul IV, Pope, 12
Paul V, Pope, 2
Paul VI, Pope, 62, 134, 149
  Draganovic and, 102
  Fátima secret and, 145
  homosexuality of, 132
  Johnson and, 133
  Martin and, 129
  St. Peter relics and, 136
  Second Vatican Council and,
    47
  Swiss Guard and, 115
  Twisted Cross staff and, 130
Pavelic, Ante "Anton," 95–96,
  98, 103
Pecorelli, Nino, 52
Pedophilia, 35–36
Penitential Bede, 36
Petawa Residence, 76
Peter, Saint, 1, 2, 23, 136
Philip IV of France (the Fair),
  17, 19–20

Philippe, Pierre Paul, 145
Pietà (Michelangelo), 27
Pike, Albert, 56
Pius IV, Pope, 36
Pius VI, Pope, 107, 117–18, 151
Pius VII, Pope, 128
Pius IX, Pope, 55, 153
Pius X, Pope, 88, 148, 153
Pius XI, Pope, 26, 30, 83, 84, 89,
  149
Pius XII, Pope (Eugenio Pacelli),
  62, 66, 99, 149
  Nazis and Hitler and, 83–91,
    94, 98, 118–19
  Soviet Union and, 57, 119–22
  UFOs and, 135
Poland, 57–58, 61–65, 71–72
Politi, Marco, 133
Pontius Pilate, 130
Pope Encyclopedia, The (Brunson),
  41–42
Popes, list of, 155–63
Popham, Peter, 55, 56–58
Pornography, 130
Printing press, 6, 7
Processus Contra Templarios (Papal
  Inquiry into the Trial of the
  Templars), 18–19
Pro Deo, 66
Propaganda Due (P2), 50, 52, 55,
  56
Protestant Reformation, 7, 9,
  128, 151

Raphael, 23, 140

Ratzinger, Joseph. *See* Benedict XVI, Pope

Rauff, Walter, 100

Reading, recommended, 183–84

Reagan, Ronald, 65–72, 133

Real estate holdings, 30

"Red tape," 2

Rentschler, James M., 67

Rerum Novarum (Of New Things), 128

Richard I of England (the Lionheart), 16

Rodino, Peter, 70

Roide, Russell J., 79

Roman Empire, 1

Romania, 119–20

Romanian Intelligence Service (DIE), 119–21

Romero, Gladys Meza, 108, 110, 112, 113–14

Roosevelt, Franklin D., 99, 133

Rosone, Roberto, 52

Rossellino, Bernardo, 2

Rowling, J.K., 14

Ruggiero, Ivan, 30

Sacramentum Poenitentiae, 36

St. Peter's Basilica, 2, 23–24, 27–28, 136–37, 139–41

Sakharovsky, Aleksandr, 119–20

Salviati, Francesco, 138

San Girolamo degli Illirici, 97–98, 102

Santos, Lúcia, 143–47

Sapieha, Adam Stefan, 61–62

Saric, Ivan, 96

Savini, Thomas M., 22

Scarafoni, Paolo, 124

Scheler, Max, 62

Sclafenato, Giovanni, 127

Scorsese, Martin, 6

"Seat-12," 120

Second Coming of Christ, 147

Second Vatican Council, 47, 62

"Secretum Omega," 135

Secret World, A (Sipe), 37–38

Seper, Francis "Franjo," 21, 145

Serbs, 95–98, 101–4

Sereny, Gitta, 100

Sergius IV, Pope, 42

Sex, Priests, and Secret Codes (Doyle, Sipe, and Wall), 39

Sexual abuse, 34–39

Sexual misbehavior, 33–39

Shea, Daniel, 35

Sicilian Mafia, 55–59, 91–93

Silvestrini, Achille, 71

Sindona, Michele, 48, 51, 52, 58, 93–94

Sipe, A.W. Richard, 37–38, 39

Sistine Chapel, 23–24, 27, 126–27

Sistine Secrets, The (Blech and Doliner), 126–27

Sixtus IV, Pope, 9, 43, 127, 151

Smith, Trevor, 54

SMOM (Sovereign Military Order of Malta), 65–66

Socci, Antonio, 146–47
Sodano, Angelo, 111
Soldiers of the Pope (documentary), 111
Solidarity (Polish trade union), 57–58, 63–65, 71–72
Somalo, Eduardo Martínez, 145
Sovereign Military Order of Malta (SMOM), 65–66
Soviet Union, 57, 63–65, 67–72, 119–22, 133
Spies in the Vatican (Alvarez and Graham), 117–18
Spinola, Giandomenico, 138
Stalin, Joseph, 57
Stanford University, 79
Stangl, Franz, 98, 100
Starry Messenger, The (Galileo), 10–11
Stephen VII, Pope, 42–43
Stephen IX, Pope, 42
Stepinac, Aloysius, 95, 104
Sterling, Claire, 69
Stowe, Harriet Beecher, 13
Summi Pontificatus, 90
Swift, Jonathan, 8
Swiss Guards, 105–16

Taylor, Myron, 133
Templars. *See* Knights Templar
Tenet, George, 111
Terror Network, The (Sterling), 69
Theodosius, 137
Thompson, Dorothy, 88

Time, 20, 44–45, 57, 64–65, 73, 74, 92, 136
Time of the Assassin, The (Sterling), 69
Tornay, Cedric, 109–15
Toth, Laszlo, 27
Truman, Harry, 133
Twisted Cross, 130

UFOs (unidentified flying objects), 134–36
Uncle Tom's Cabin (Stowe), 13
Unholy Trinity (Aarons and Loftus), 92, 99
United Nations World Magazine, 25
University of Notre Dame, 79–80
Urban II, Pope, 15
Urban VIII, Pope, 11
U.S. Federal Reserve Bank, 25
Ustashi (Ustase), 95–96, 97–98, 101–3

Valentinian II, 36
Varisco, Antonio, 52
Vatican Bank, 48, 50–51, 52, 55, 57–58, 59, 94, 101–4
Vatican Billions, The (Manhattan), 24–25
Vatican Exposed, The (Williams), 91–92
Vatican Gendarmerie, 115
Vatican Library, 8–10, 130–31
    chronology, 151–52

Vatican Museums, 26–29
Vatican Secret Archives, 2–3
  chronology, 153
Vergès, Jacques, 115
Verkaik, Robert, 55, 56–58
Vicarius Filii Dei, 131
Vicars of Christ (de Rosa), 43
Villa Giula, 127
Villot, Jean-Marie, 46, 48–49,
  50–51
Vittor, Silvano, 58–59

Wagner, Gustav, 100
Wagner, Robert F., Jr., 133
Walesa, Lech, 63–64
Wall, Patrick J., 39
Wall Street Journal, 25, 134
Walters, Vernon, 66
Washington Monthly, 80
Weizsacker, Ernst von, 118
Westfield Residence, 76
Wiesenthal, Simon, 100
Willan, Philip, 55, 56–58
William of Tyre, 16–17

Williams, Paul L., 92
Willows School, 76
Wilson, William, 67, 71
Wilson, Woodrow, 132
Windmoor Residence, 76
Windswept House: A Vatican Novel
  (Martin), 129
Wingren Residence, 76
Wojtyła, Karol. *See* John Paul II,
  Pope
Wolf, Hubert, 6, 83
Woodward, Kenneth, 77
World War I, 118, 144
World War II, 66–67, 81, 144
  the papacy and the Nazis,
    83–94, 98–100, 107, 118–22
  spooks and rats, 95–104
Wurstemberg, Hugues de, 111
Wyszynski, Stefan, 62

Yallop, David, 50–51, 80–81
Yalta Conference, 71–72

Ziemann, George Patrick, 37